Auriculas

Auriculas

Gwen Baker & Peter Ward

B.T. Batsford Ltd • London

First published 1995

© Peter Ward, Gwen Baker 1995

Typeset and designed by David Seabourne
and printed in Hong Kong

Published by
B.T. Batsford Ltd
4 Fitzhardinge Street
London W1H 0AH

A catalogue record for this book is available
from the British Library

ISBN 0 7134 7366 5

Contents

27. 'Beckminster' Gold-centred Alpine auricula (photo G. Baker)
28. 'Sirius' Light-centred Alpine auricula
29. 'Lee Paul' Light-centred Alpine auricula
30. 'Sandra' Light-centred Alpine auricula
31. 'Mikado' Self show auricula (photo G. Baker)
32. 'Remus' Self show auricula (photo G. Baker)
33. 'Tracy Ward' Self show auricula
34. 'April Moon' Self show auricula
35. 'Brompton' Self show auricula (photo G. Baker)
36. 'Upton Belle' Self show auricula (photo G. Baker)
37. 'Moonglow' Self show auricula
38. 'Cherry' Self show auricula (photo Dr D. A. Duthie)
39. 'Golden Chartreuse' Double auricula
40. 'Diamond' Double auricula
41. 'Westcott Pride' Double auricula
42. 'Koh-i-noor' Double auricula (photo M. Sheader)
43. 'Thirlmere' Double auricula (photo M. Sheader)
44. 'Gaia' Double auricula (photo M. Sheader)
45. Seedling double auriculas raised by Dr M. Sheader (photo M. Sheader)
46. 'Jane Myers' Double auricula (photo G. Baker)
47. 'Susannah' Double auricula
48. 'Pink Fondant' Double auricula (photo G. Baker)
49. 'Gingernut' Double auricula
50. 'Sarah Brightman' Double auricula
51. 'Raleigh Stripe' Striped show auricula (photo C. A. Hawkes)
52. 'May Tiger' Striped show auricula (photo C. A. Hawkes)
53. Yellow ground fancy show auricula
54. 'Spaceage' Fancy show auricula
55. Seedling border auricula
56. 'Bellamy Pride' Border auricula
57. 'Rusty Red' Border auricula
58. Red garden auricula
59. Seedling border
60. Borders on show bench, centre 'Mrs Harris'

All photographs by P. G. Ward except where noted

Acknowledgements

Although between us we have over fifty years experience in growing auriculas no two people have a monopoly of knowledge on their chosen subject. This book would not have been possible without the willing co-operation of colleagues and friends, all of whom are members of the National Auricula and Primula Society (N.A.P.S.). They answered our many requests for information in a generous, unstinting manner and also gave us every encouragement.

Our deepest thanks therefore to: Len Bailey, Brian Coop, Tim Coop, Arthur Delbridge, John Gibson, Allan Guest, David Hadfield, Penny Harrison, Allan Hawkes, Ike Hawthorn, Keith Leeming, Trevor Newton, Geoff Nicolle, Eddie Picken, the late Charles Rennie, Derek Salt, Martin Sheader, Derek Telford, Cliff Timpson, Ken Whorton and Lawrence Wigley.

We should also like to thank David Tarver for producing the excellent line drawings in this volume and Howard Drury for his encouragement and advice.

Finally we would like to thank Jennifer Ward for assistance in producing and checking the manuscript and Bob Archdale for spending many hours reading it and offering constructive criticism and advice.

Peter Ward, Gwen Baker

Introduction

Auriculas are members of the genus *Primula*, a vast assembly of over 400 wild species and many hybrids, including our native primroses, cowslips and the hybrid between them, from which has been developed the polyanthus. Primulas take their name from the Latin name for primroses and cowslips, *Primula veris*, which has the charming translation of 'the first little thing of spring', the Latin 'primus' meaning first. They were written about by the herbalist, John Gerard, who lists them, along with the oxlip, under the same name. When in 1753 Carolus Linnaeus published his *Species Plantarum* setting out the bi-nominal system of naming plants and animals, he bestowed this name on the cowslip, calling the common primrose *Primula vulgaris*. There is a number of primula species growing wild in the Alps and it is believed that two, *Primula auricula* and *Primula hirsuta*, were cross-pollinated to form the natural hybrid, usually called *Primula* x *pubescens*, which can still be found growing wild in the mountains. It is also believed that modern auriculas are descended from this hybrid and are classified scientifically under this name. Gwen Baker has made pilgrimages to see all three of these plants growing wild, high in the Alps, only between 3,000–8,000 ft (1,000–2,500 m) above the tree line, always in rocky places.

Tradition has it that before 1583 peasants found this hybrid growing on the mountains 'beyond Innsbruck' and that the plants found their way in due course to the gardens of the Hapsburg Emperor, Maximilian II and to his court botanist Charles l'Ecluse, better known by his Latin name Clusius. He had his own garden in Vienna and attempted to grow several species of wild primulas among other plants. Clusius wrote a book telling of his attempts and states he was most successful at 'taming' *Primula ursi*, now believed to be the yellow *Primula auricula* and a second plant he called *Primula ursi II*. From his description of it we now believe this was the introduction of *Primula* x *pubescens* into cultivation. Many species of wild European primulas are in cultivation today and can be grown successfully, although it is sometimes difficult to get them to flower. In due course Clusius returned to his native Low Countries, becoming Professor of Botany at Leyden University, probably bringing his auriculas with him. Certainly their cultivation spread to Belgium and in due course to Britain. The first English description of auriculas was in 1597, in John Gerard's *Herbal* where he describes seven varieties of 'Beare's Ears', yellow, purple, blush and three shades of red.

Over the years we have learned of the time and dedication given by many in fashioning these plants. They have the neat perfection of man-made artefacts but are living plants. The dedicated band who grow them call themselves 'Florists' and their charges are called 'Florists' auriculas'.

Today 'florist' is usually taken to mean someone who sells flowers from a shop but that is not the way it is used in this book, rather it is used with the original meaning of 'one who attempts to grow flowers to perfection'. Men first grew plants for utilitarian ends, for food or other purposes, such as for their medicinal properties, for 'strewing herbs', for fragrance and for seasoning. People who grew plants for these useful properties, especially for medicine, were and indeed are still called 'herbalists'. When people began to have time and leisure to spare they began growing plants for their beauty and their scent, at about the time of Elizabeth I in Britain.

It coincided with an influx of plants from abroad like tulips, carnations and auriculas. People who grew them became known as florists to distinguish them from herbalists, and in due course the term became more specialized, referring to those who tried to improve and perfect their blooms, testing their prowess in competitions with fellow enthusiasts. Our modern florists are as likely to grow roses, begonias, chrysanthemums or fuchsias, but the growers of auriculas, tulips, carnations and other old-fashioned flowers were the original florists. The old meaning of the term is still used to differentiate the highly selected plants used for formal exhibition from the simple unspecialized plants available for general garden decoration. People who grew flowers for sale were originally called 'market florists' but in time the word 'market' was dropped from general speech.

The devotees of the auricula have banded together in the National Auricula and Primula Society (N.A.P.S.), with three Sections; the Northern Section centred in Lancashire and Yorkshire with a group in Northumberland; the Midland and West Section with shows in Birmingham and Bristol, and the Southern Section who hold their shows in London. We have attended the centenary shows of two of these Sections, while the third, the Midland and West, are already planning their centenary show in AD 2000.

During the two World Wars this century the number of adherents to the auricula fell severely. However through the expertise and dedication of the Society members the plants survived and over the last twenty years the numbers of growers, nurseries selling them and number of varieties have increased steadily, as more and more people are becoming involved in growing and hybridizing. New varieties are continually being bred, mostly by amateur members of the Society and are distributed to those known to be capable of growing them – often through plants sales at the various meetings. Many fine plants are not generally available to the wider public nor are they sold by ordinary garden centres. To some they are living antiques and like antiques they are hunted and collected, cherished and displayed.

This book tells of their cultivation, of the different types of auricula, how they differ one from another and how they may be collected and cultivated.

1 The Origins of Florists' Auriculas

It is believed that Florists' auriculas are descended from the hybrid between *Primula auricula* and *Primula hirsuta*. As the hybrid has characteristics from both ancestors we will consider features of both these plants and the way these characteristics are combined, both in the original hybrid and in the more sophisticated modern auricula.

THE WILD ANCESTORS

Primula auricula is a high-Alpine plant growing above the treeline, usually on ledges or rocky limestone outcrops in the Alps. It grows over a wide area, stretching from the French Alps and the German Black Forest in the west, to the Tatra and Carpathian mountains in the east. This is a vast range and it is not surprising perhaps that there is much variation, some plants having a powdering of farina or meal, a white powdery waxy substance (explained on p. 15), on their leaves. Most varieties also have a powdering of this farina round the eye of the yellow trumpet-shaped flowers, which grow in a cluster on the top of a footstalk, similar at first glance to the cowslip. Indeed the wild auricula has been called the 'mountain cowslip' although its leaves are different in shape and texture, pointed like an animal's ear. They are thicker and more leathery than cowslip leaves, almost succulent, more able to withstand cold frosts, biting winds and heat. The leaves are carried on a stout, branching rhizome and occur in clusters or crowns. It is from these pointed leaves that the plant takes its old Latin name, *Auricula ursi* which translates as 'little ear of a bear'.

The yellow pigment, flavin, that colours the flowers appears in a thin layer near the surface of the petals. *Primula auricula* is a saxatile plant, i.e. it grows in rocky places, on boulders and ledges, less frequently on high stony meadows. These are invariably places where other larger plants do not smother it and the drainage is superb. It is a high alpine rarely occurring below 3,000 ft (1,000 m). Gwen Baker saw a fine example on a mountaineering and plant-hunting holiday in Switzerland. To photograph it she had to lie down on the turf. The plant grew in front of a boulder behind which was a 1,000 ft (300 m) drop to the valley below!

Another old name for the plant is the '*schwindelkraut*', or 'giddiness plant' and indeed it would have been dangerous to photograph it close up standing upright. In his *Herbal* (1597) Gerard wrote: 'the root ... is in great request for the strengthening of the head, that when they are on the top of places that are high, giddiness and the swimming of the braine may not affect them'. We suppose this comes from the 'doctrine of the signatures', when the old herbalists believed every plant was put on earth for man's benefit and its use was evident from the plant itself; presumably here by the lofty positions in which it grew.

Primula auricula shows considerable variation within its range and two subspecies and several clones have been named. Subspecies *P. auricula bauhini* is taken as the typical form, with leaves that may or may not carry farina, with short cilia or hairs round the leaf margins and lemon-yellow scented flowers. *P. auricula albocincta* has particularly dense farina on the leaf margins, and another clone *P. auricula albocincta nuda* has farina in the throat of the flower. Yet another has toothed leaves, while a second subspecies *P. auricula ciliata* has no farina and deep-yellow flowers without scent. These variations are also found in the hybrid auriculas.

The second parent, *Primula hirsuta*, normally grows on acid rocks, although it is occasionally found on limestone where vegetation has collected and decayed into an acid layer. It too has a wide range, in the Pyrenees as well as right across the Alps. It is a smaller plant with tufts of green sticky leaves bearing microscopic red hairs that give off a characteristic pungent smell. This has been likened at times to the smell of 'old goat' and the whole plant is devoid of farina. It does not like sunshine or competition and grows mainly on north facing cliffs and boulders, seaming the cracks and fissures, with roots embedded in moss and crevices. Occasionally it grows on high moorland, such as Alp Grum in the Engadine region of Switzerland, where it covers the ground like grass, so densely that you are forced to tread on the plants as there is nowhere else to put your feet.

The flowers are flat and round, unlike the trumpet shape of *Primula auricula*, and of varying shades of pink, red and purple. The pigment that colours these flowers is called 'hirsutin' and has the ability to change colour according to the acidity of the sap, in the

same way as litmus paper. Consequently there is a wide range of shades in this species, depending on the concentration of the pigment and the sap acidity, from palest pink to deep purple, near black. Under a microscope it can be seen that the rosy pigment is contained in a series of cells in the middle of the petal, shaped very much like pears. The broad end is uppermost with a thickening on the top, as we are told in a fascinating little book, *The Auricula* by Sir Roland Biffen.

Both these ancestral plants flower in the mountain spring, with the melting of the snows, when the high hills seep moisture and the turf is like a sponge. Wherever limestone and acid rock come together, their hybrid may still be found. A friend of Gwen Baker told her that he saw a group of hybrids, where acid rock and limestone met and a whole range of colours were present from cream to brown. She also found a hybrid growing within a big patch of wild *Primula auricula*, a squat unattractive flower of brilliant magenta and photographed it. It is strange to reflect that a similar unattractive flower may have been an ancestor of the beautiful hybrids we grow now.

PRIMULA x PUBESCENS, THE HYBRID

Primula x *pubescens*, the 'downy primrose', is still in cultivation, usually as a rock garden plant.

Scientifically, all of the many hybrid 'auriculas' grown today should be known by this name. The plant, smaller than auriculas proper, usually has small trumpet-shaped flowers: yellow, red or purple, growing in profusion. It blossoms in the spring over small rosettes of pointed leaves, which in a year or two form thick clumps.

It can inherit either the yellow or red pigment, or both. Pigment is carried in separate layers in the petals, so the flowers can be found in a rainbow of colours including white, only true blue missing. *Primula* x *pubescens* has more colour potential than almost any other flower, except for the related polyanthus and the well-named rainbow plant, the iris.

The leaves of *P.* x *pubescens* may or may not be mealy, usually not, as the gene for meal is recessive and if present may be masked. The meal may also be found as a ring in the eye of the flower but is often absent. Examples of present-day varieties are plants such as 'Faldonside', 'Mrs J. H. Wilson' and 'Carmen', known also as *P.* x *pubescens* 'Boothman's variety'. Apart from their diminutive size they are similar to border auriculas. Occasionally the flowers are more trumpet-shaped and indeed in the larger, flatter plants like 'Rufus' and 'Chamois', it is difficult to know where the dividing line lies. At shows these two varieties have been exhibited in different classes, both as border auriculas and as *P.* x *pubescens*. In general, varieties of *P.* x *pubescens* are regarded for show purposes as hardy primula hybrids and make excellent plants for pans, trough gardens and small rock gardens, happiest in slight shade with shelter from hot sun. They are evergreen, hardy and floriferous, growing into ever-widening clumps. The clumps are best split, when necessary, just after flowering, before the heat of summer develops and they need protecting from slugs and snails.

PARTS OF THE AURICULA

This book is about Florists' auriculas and we now give a brief general description and explanation of the many technical or cant terms in common use, before going on to place the plants in their various classes.

Auriculas are small herbaceous plants, with one or more whorls or 'crowns' of leaves, growing at the top of a short stout rhizome, or 'carrot' from which the roots emerge. The roots are of two types, long thong roots that serve to anchor the plant to the ground, and growing from them finer feeding roots. The latter spread through the soil to supply the plant with water and mineral salts. New plantlets arise from the main carrot which soon develop their own root system. Once this has occurred they are ready to be removed as 'Irishmen's cuttings' and grown separately. These small separated plantlets are known as 'offsets'. If left undivided they soon form a small cluster of crowns, or a clump, as do polyanthus; this clump forming can be well observed in border auriculas in many suburban gardens. Left undivided the outer-most rhizomes fall sideways and develop roots where they touch the surface.

The leaves are evergreen but reduce in the winter to the tight folded 'resting-buds' found in most types of primula. Some primulas leave these winter resting buds above ground while others withdraw below and one does not know for certain exactly where the plant is, or indeed if it is still alive until it reappears in spring. The resting-buds of auriculas remain above ground and clearly visible. In this tightly-furled state the plant is dormant and able to withstand the rigours of winter. We believe it is during the dormant condition that flower buds are initiated, although others think this occurs in autumn. The unwanted leaves die down and decay in the garden but in the greenhouse dry out to small crisp bodies that should be removed. They spoil the appearance of the plant and may attract mould spores.

The flowers are similar in bearing to the polyanthus but the leaves are very different,

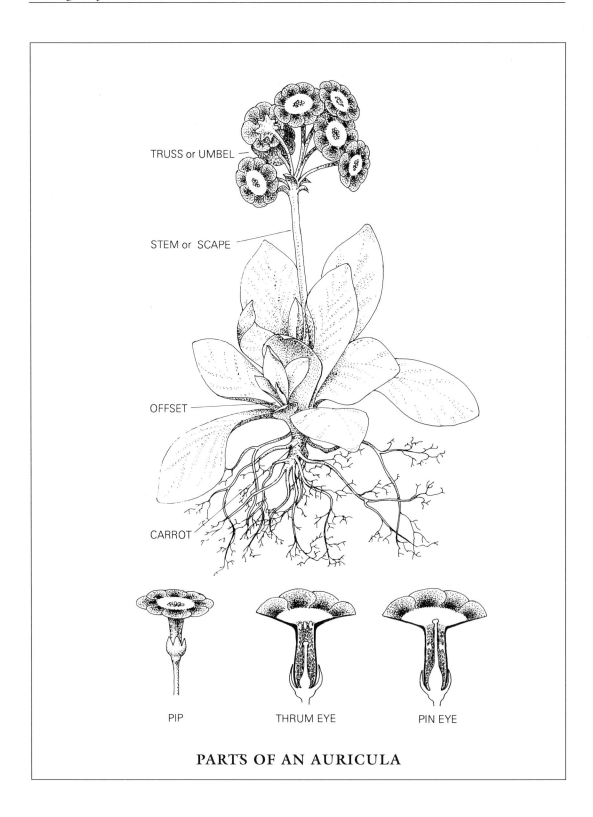

TRUSS or UMBEL

STEM or SCAPE

OFFSET

CARROT

PIP

THRUM EYE

PIN EYE

PARTS OF AN AURICULA

rather succulent, thick and leathery, with a smooth waxy surface and pointed like the ear of a bear or a cat. Some have small serrations on the edge, usually on the top half of the leaf — they are 'toothed'. They may have layers or patches covered by glandular hairs, which secrete drops of a white waxy substance, known as 'farina' or 'meal'. Under a microscope these hairs can be seen clearly, although invisible to the unaided eye, as can the drops of white wax they exude. Strangely, farina is not present on juvenile leaves, and it is quite normal to have a mature plant, white with farina, ringed by green-leaved offsets. This is an important point since plants are normally distributed as small offsets. A new grower might imagine they had the wrong plant if they were unaware of this characteristic.

The degree of whiteness imparted by farina differs, depending on the variety, from a light frosting to a layer completely covering the leaves, giving a white or grey appearance. Another old name for auriculas is 'dusty millers'. The purpose of farina is unknown but it is very decorative and can be found in different places on a number of other primulas. In many, including the wild auricula, there is a ring of farina round the centre tube or 'eye' of the flower. This feature has been exploited and developed in the show auricula, as will be explained later. On and around the eye of the flower the farina is known as 'paste'.

As farina is an exudation, not attached to the plant, rain causes it to run and even completely wash off, so to protect their beauty show auriculas are normally grown under glass, at least until after flowering.

The flowers arise in late spring, in April or early May, from the crown. Each crown may bear one or two umbels, or 'trusses'. The individual flowers in the truss are flat or very slightly trumpet-shaped, larger than the flow-

ers of *P. pubescens* and borne on a strong stem which raises the flowers above the leaves. This makes them visible to bees and other pollinating insects, that are also attracted to the flower by a sweet perfume.

The flatness of the flower, inherited from *P. hirsuta*, is a point of perfection in the eyes of the judge. The cant name for the individual floret is 'pip' and each pip has its own pedicel or 'footstalk' joining it to the main stem of the truss, all at one position where there is usually a small bract or 'guardleaf'. The number of flowers are variable from two or three to over twenty, according to nutrition and genetic inheritance. In nature the flowers are of two kinds, 'pin-eyed' and 'thrum-eyed'.

PINS AND THRUMS

Most primulas use a device, technically known as dimorphism, meaning 'two forms', to promote cross-pollination and the widest possible variation in the seedlings, and the auricula is no exception. 'Thrum-eyed' flowers have the stamens, bearing the male pollen, in a ring at the throat of the flower. They were thought by the old growers, many of whom were weavers, to resemble the little cut ends of thread left when the woven web was cut off the loom, so were given the old weaving term of 'thrums'; the plant where they were visible being 'thrum-eyed'.

Lower down the floral tube is the style, which is shaped like a dressmaker's pin, with a little knob. The stigma, the receptive female part, is on the end of a short column, the style in turn connected to the ovary or seedbox. In the 'pin-eyed' flower the positions are reversed, the pin-shaped stigma visible in the throat of the flower and the stamens hidden deep in the floral tube in the middle of the flower.

To aid in the cross-pollination of the seeds the stigma is receptive before the pollen on that flower ripens, reducing the possibility of self-pollination. It has recently been shown by electron microscope pictures that the size of the cavities in the stigma surface and of the pollen grains differ in the two sorts of flowers. The size of 'thrum' pollen exactly fits the grooves in 'pin' stigmas and vice versa. Charles Darwin informed us that in most primulas, like our native primrose, a pin/thrum cross gives 100 per cent germination, while like x like, e.g. thrum x thrum gives few fertile seeds, about 5 per cent. However, auricula growers decided a couple of centuries ago that pin-eyed flowers, or 'pips' as the individual florets are known, have a 'curious vacant appearance, displeasing to the human eye' and pin-eyes still carry an automatic disqualification on the show bench.

For over two centuries at least hybridizers have discarded pin-eyed plants and selected those with thrums. The majority of thrums bear seeds regularly if crossed with another thrum-eyed plant. Thus, over the years the biological barriers must have, to some extent, been broken down. 'To some extent' because the highly prized 'edged' varieties are sometimes reluctant to bear seed, even if hand-pollinated. Often the seed pods develop but on ripening are found to be empty. Even if seed is formed and sown it does not always germinate, although this may be due to faulty sowing techniques.

Another trait that seems to be hereditary is the relative toughness and longevity of the individual variety. Some are incredibly long-lived. One Alpine variety, 'Argus', is known from our records to have been shown as a seedling in 1890, over a century ago, so it must have germinated at least two years previously. It is still winning prizes on the show bench and survives happily as a garden plant of more recent planting.

Many other named varieties are known from the turn of the century, although few are Show auriculas, and Border auriculas are regularly reputed to have come from grandparents' gardens. However, the reverse is also true: many varieties are shown as seedlings, win prizes and are named but last only a few years before they die out. One example is a most beautiful double auricula named 'Ivory'. Offsets were passed on, as insurance against loss, to other seasoned growers but in a few years all had died, something that must be put down to a poor constitution. Today, only a photograph remains.

Ability to offset freely seems to be another inherited factor. 'Argus', cited above for its longevity, produces offsets freely and even the smallest ones, if they originate from below the soil, have an incredibly long root. On the other hand, some varieties noted for their good form and winning properties, like the gold-centre Alpine auricula 'Largo', offset reluctantly, barely reproducing before the adult plant dies. Consequently this variety is in short supply and eagerly sort after. Here it may be a suitable place to inform readers that in general one plant lasts about four to six years, exceptionally ten, and the continuance of that variety in a collection depends on a supply of young offsets. Many of the best growers would contend that plants need replacing after three to five years at least. Border auriculas die in the middle while the new side growths root down into the soil. The first flowering truss from a seedling is known as a 'maiden truss' and the old plant from which offsets have been taken at repotting is called a 'stag'. Why plants are supposed to change sex with age is not known, as they are in any case hermaphrodites, both sexes being present in the same flower.

TYPES OF AURICULA

Striped

Show
Circle of Paste

Alpine

Self

Edged

Fancy

One Colour - Unshaded

Body Colour
usually Black

Body Colour
Other than Black

Green Edge

Grey Edge

White Edge

No Meal on Petals

Some Meal on Petals

Thick Meal on Petals

TYPES OF FLORISTS' AURICULA

Over the centuries several different types of auriculas have been developed. Gardeners have always looked for the new and unusual and this is certainly the case with auriculas. Plants that show different characteristics are seized upon and crossed with others to see if a new exciting generation can be created. Recently, an Alpine seedling called 'Sirius' was introduced with shading much more pronounced than usual. This has given us a new colour break in Alpines and many excellent seedlings, of which 'Lee Paul' is the best known example, have been shown in recent years.

This must have happened in the past when doubles, stripes and the fabulous edged varieties made their first appearances. From these early times criteria were laid down which new seedlings had to meet to gain acceptance, these criteria including symmetry and pure colouring. A misshapen flower or one of a muddy colour were cast aside as not good enough, only the best being retained. Even so the plants had to be exhibited on the show bench against those from other hybridizers and only the winners would be in demand. Our flowers today show the results of this process of selection and are divided into five groups.

The main divide is the presence or absence of paste in the eye of the flower, those with farina being known as Show auriculas, which are sub-divided into Edged varieties and Selfs, i.e. all one colour apart from the eye. None of the other sections, Alpines, Double and Borders have this paste eye, though some borders have a thin ring of farina round the eye, as has the ancestral *P. auricula*. Doubles also sometimes show traces of farina but it is obscured by the extra petals and meal is often more obvious on the back of the pips.

SHOW AURICULAS

Show auriculas are considered by many the aristocrats of the auricula world and have a ring of dense farina, the paste, round the eye of the flower. At the beginning of the century only Show auriculas were allowed on the show bench, hence their name. As the farina can be spoiled by one drop of rain, causing it to run, they are normally grown under cover to protect this unique feature. They are sub-divided into selfs, all one colour and edged varieties. These sections are again subdivided into other sub-sections.

Selfs

Self-coloured auriculas are usually either red, yellow, auricula blue, which is really a kind of purple, and very dark red where the colour is so concentrated the flower appears black. Only the best unshaded flowers are named and have a golden tube surrounded by dense white paste, the contrasting colours being most striking. Any colours that do not fit into the above classification have a special class provided, 'any other colour'. Lately this has been enlarged with many new colours appearing, for instance brown.

Edged Auriculas

Edged auriculas are some of the most remarkable flowers in cultivation today; the outside edge of the pip replaced by leaf tissue, which may or may not have the farina bearing hairs on it. If no farina is present, the plant is a 'green-edge', if a light smattering of white farina partly masks the green the resultant flower appears grey and we have the 'grey-edge'; if the farina is so dense as to completely mask the green, the result is a 'white-edged' flower. As the amount of farina increases, the size of the flower decreases, so that green-edges are the largest and white-edges the smallest.

The appearance of these flowers with golden tube and band of pure white paste is unique. The only variation allowed in the flower is a band of colour, known as the ground or 'ground-colour', between the paste and the green, grey or white edge. Today the accepted colour is black, or as near black as possible. It occurs in a band, the inside edge next to the paste, smooth and completely circular but on the outside edge streaks out in an irregular feathery fashion; 'flashing out' is the cant phrase. However, it must never flash out to the rim of the flower, breaking up the continuity of the green edge. Any flower where the ground-colour does flash out to the edge is faulty and may be relegated, providing it has some attraction, to the Fancy class, or indeed discarded.

Fancy Auriculas

Fancy auriculas are basically 'failed' edged varieties, either because their ground-colour flashes out too far, or because they do not have the accepted black ground. The form of these plants, in present-day varieties, is invariably inferior to the black-bodied plants and mitigates against them. We know from previous records, around 1820, body colours of red, yellow, purple and brown were considered acceptable in edged auriculas, and very striking they must have been with the white paste and green or grey edges. Why black became the accepted colour is not known although it does provide a striking contrast. Some growers would like to see coloured-ground edged flowers admitted to the top classes. This will depend on seedlings being introduced that have better form than the ragged specimens common today. Improvement in form is something that is being worked on at present by, amongst others, Tim Coop of Harrogate.

One judge is quoted as saying he could not 'abear the Fancies, as they don't obey the rules' and for that reason he would not judge them. Many can be striking, particularly yellow-ground greens and purple-ground greys. They tend to be favourites with new growers, perhaps because they are easier to obtain and to recognize. To the untrained eye many of the uniformly black-ground edged plants look very similar, though experts can identify them at a glance.

Striped Auriculas

Striped auriculas have recently made a comeback after being lost to cultivation for over 100 years. We know they were favourites before the arrival of the edged varieties, around 1750, but they then became unfashionable and were no longer grown and so died out. About twenty-five years ago the well known grower and hybridist, Allan Hawkes, of Rabley Heath in Hertfordshire, applied himself to the task and stripes have returned. They are still rare but other raisers are now using Allan's material and creating more and more varieties. The stripes are farina on coloured petals in the modern seedlings, but old illustrations show purple on yellow and other strange combinations which have yet to reappear.

Border Auriculas

Border auriculas are the nearest to the ancestral types, prized for their toughness and ability to maintain themselves in the garden and for their sweet scent. They are larger than the *pubescens* types and generally have flat flowers, often with a faint farinose eye.

Alpine Auriculas

Alpine auriculas have no trace of farina on leaves or flower and their flower colour shades out from the deepest, next to the tube, to a lighter colouring on the outer edge. The tube shows the basic colour of the pip and various shades on top give the many lovely colours in this section, which depends to a great extent on this ground-colour: gold, white or cream. Obviously shades of red on a gold ground give deeper, richer colours than red on a white ground, where the colours are in general lighter and more delicate. As the concentration of the pigment in the sap and its acidity vary from flower to flower, many wonderful shades are found and the two layers of cells in which the colour pigments occur give a deep velvety richness to the texture. There are then two sections, the gold-centres and the light-centres; the latter including white and cream.

Gold centres are generally dark red shading to bright red, or shades of brown shading to gold.

Light centres are usually two shades of near blue, red becoming pink, or purple shading to mauve. Some of the deeper, more intense colours are more highly prized as they are uncommon, while other seedlings fail because the shading is not noticeable enough.

At one time unshaded Alpines formed a separate group and were known as Alpine selfs or 'pures'. Such plants are not considered acceptable today and are relegated to the garden or border auricula group.

Double Auriculas

Double auriculas have only been rediscovered in the past forty years and are still being developed. Consensus on shape is still not formed, some raisers and judges favouring fuller, heavier flowers, while others prefer the doubles with lighter less full flowers, though all agree petals must cover the centre, making the tube invisible. Colour can vary from almost white, through cream, yellow and gold to browns, gingers and chestnuts and there are also a large number of purples and wine reds. True scarlets are as yet unavailable but some recent seedlings of crimson, with no blue in them, are promising. There is great scope for improvement in both form and flower colouring with clearer brighter colours needed. A most exciting group to our minds, as there is so much scope for breeders.

2 Show Auriculas

The moment of first seeing a show auricula is an experience rarely forgotten. Nature and generations of enthusiasts have combined to produce a flower with a unique combination of symmetry, texture and colour. The fascination is such that for those who grow them it can never be a passing fancy and frequently develops into a lifelong hobby.

The show auricula is divided into two distinct types, selfs and edged (see illustrations). Both have a circle of paste or farina and for selfs a corolla of one colour. The paste is very delicate and is easily smeared. The green-edged varieties have meal-free foliage whereas most of the others, both grey edges and selfs, have a covering of meal or farina on the leaves that varies in density. These 'mealed' types require careful handling so as not to spoil the appearance of the foliage. The edged varieties are prized by many above all others and are subdivided into green, grey and white-edged. In addition we have fancies and stripes, the latter, very popular in earlier centuries but lost, until their reintroduction very recently, after an extensive breeding programme by Allan Hawkes of Rabley Heath, Hertfordshire.

STANDARDS OF PERFECTION

The standards of perfection for show auriculas are very precisely defined. While general agreement exists on many features of the flower the proportions are another matter. Two principle standards have held sway since the early eighteenth century. The first to be introduced was by J. Maddock in *The Florists' Directory*, published in 1792. Maddock defined the proportions of the flower regarding the tube, paste and petal width, summarized as a ratio of 6:3:1. Somewhat later, in 1832, George Glenny, a prolific writer of the period, advocated a different set of proportions, which became known as 'Glenny's Rules', reducing them to a 4:2:1 ratio. While attempts have occasionally been made to introduce alternatives Maddock and Glenny remain unchallenged, each having its advocates. Generally more varieties seem closer to the Glenny formula than that of Maddock, although the Northern growers are vociferous advocates of Maddock's, especially with regard to his smaller tube. The precise definitions are:

MADDOCK 1792: 'The component parts of the pip are the tube, the eye and the exterior circle. These three should be well proportioned, which will be the case if the diameter of the tube be one part, the eye three, and the whole pip six, or nearly so.'

GLENNY 1832: 'The proportions of the flower may be described by drawing four circles round a given point at equal

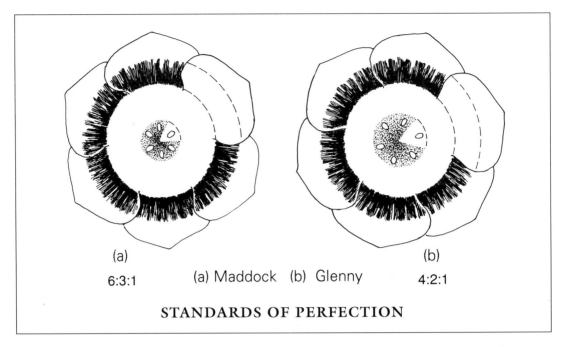

(a)

6:3:1

(a) Maddock (b) Glenny

(b)

4:2:1

STANDARDS OF PERFECTION

distances; the first circle forming the tube, the second the white eye, the third the ground colour, and the fourth the outer edge of the flower, and the nearer they approximate to this the better the flower.'

Florists' Auriculas and Gold Laced Polyanthus, *c.*1957 by C. G. Haysom, gave the following extract from the Royal Horticultural Society's Paper No. 38.

AURICULA SHOW

MERITORIOUS Well-balanced, crisp, healthy foliage. A strong stem, sufficiently long to bear the truss well above the foliage. A truss consisting of not fewer than five fully developed pips (three in seedlings) carried on peduncles sufficiently long to avoid overlapping of the pips. A perfectly flat, round, smooth-edged pip consisting of six or more lobes, without notches or serrations. A circular tube with a diameter approximately equal to one-sixth of the pip, slightly raised at the edge of the paste, of a deep yellow colour, and filled by the anthers, hiding the stigma. A pure white, smooth paste, free from crack or blemish, circular in outline, and of a width equal to that of the ground colour and edge together. A dense ground colour, forming a perfect circle near the paste, the darker and richer the colour the better, though red should not be regarded as a fault. A bright green, grey or white edge of about the same width as the ground colour. In selfs the colour should be uniform throughout and without shading. The paste should be as required in the edged section and should be about equal in width to that of the border colour.

DEFECTIVE Foliage which is ill-balanced, limp or unhealthy. A stem that is weak or short. A truss that has fewer than five well developed pips (fewer than three in a seedling) or has peduncles that are too short to prevent overlapping of the pips. A pip that is not flat, circular or smooth edged, or has fewer than six lobes. A tube that is irregular, or has a diameter exceeding one-sixth of that of the pip, or is pale coloured, or has a visible stigma. A paste that is not pure white, or is rough, cracked or blemished, or lacks a circular outline, or is of a width that is not approximately equal to that of the combined ground-colour and edge. A ground-colour that has not a perfectly circular outline, or is wider than half the width of the paste, or that lacks density or richness. An edge that is not self-coloured or that is wider than half the width of the paste.

Scale for show auriculas other than selfs

Foliage, stem and truss	7 points
Pip	2 points
Tube	2 points
Paste	3 points
Ground-colour	3 points
Edge	3 points
	20

Scale for selfs

Foliage, stem and truss	7 points
Pip	4 points
Tube	3 points
Centre	3 points
Edge	3 points
	20'

Haysom also quoted the score points drawn up by his friend Dan Bamford of Middleton, Lancashire, considered a great authority on the auricula.

'1. *Tube* Rich yellow, circular, outer edge level with expanded pip — 10 points.
2. *Anthers* Dense, curving evenly inwards covering the stigma — 10 points.
3. *Paste* Smooth and dense, free from cracks, centre circular, meal in grey-edged variety dense enough to be pure white without showing any green petal. Green-edged variety free from meal and preferably dark green — 25 points.
4. *Body* Colour circular where it joins the centre, feathering a little into the edge colour (body colour preferably black) — 15 points.
5. *Stem and footstalk* Stem strong enough to carry the truss well above the foliage and rigid enough to allow each pip to display itself without overcrowding — 10 points.
6. *Pip* Round and flat, no notches in petals, six to seven petals in a flower, colour zones of equal width — 20 points.
7. *Size, substance and general refinement* — 10 points.'

Whether the body colour should be confined to black remains contentious and there are many who would wish to see other colours reintroduced. Bamford also stated a preference for a dark-green edge that is another point on which we would take issue.

In reality modern judges do not use a points system, time not permitting, and reach their decisions based on experience and knowledge of the plants. The points system can be used with benefit by raisers of new seedlings providing they are not dogmatic; seedlings can vary enormously in the first few years.

GREEN-EDGED

Virescent forms of flowers, while not common, do exist in a variety of different plants. Indeed this is so with both the double auricula and primrose but few are other than interesting curiosities. This is not true of the green-edged auricula that is now highly developed and in its present form much changed from the early mutations. Exactly how this came about we do not know except that the first edged plants appeared in about 1740. The normal petals were replaced by structures identical with the foliage leaves. The edged auricula had arrived and the florists of the day were soon introducing a large variety of flowers, which also included the grey or white types.

In the greens the colour shade varies, although in most other varieties differences are small. A few, 'Jupiter' being a good example, are noticeably lighter and some growers find this more attractive. In 'Jupiter' the lighter edge combines with a yellow tube and white paste to give a brighter effect than those of the darker greens.

Usually the pips of greens are larger than those of other edged varieties and most selfs. They should be completely without farina and the 'china edged' flowers of the old florists are not acceptable to today's judges. 'China edged' flowers refer to plants with farina outlining the margins of the petals. One problem with green-edges is that they are comparatively short-lived. The oldest known variety still being grown is 'Tinkerbell', raised in 1932 by Clive Cookson of Nether Warden, Northumberland; in fact 'Tinkerbell' was raised by his gardener W. J. Stables. Cookson was a coal owner in the days before nationalisation when it was not uncommon for some of the famous auricula growers of the day to employ gardeners. He was also given credit for raising the original seedlings that led to today's blues but again it was W. J. Stables we should thank. We know this because Peter Ward's father, then a young apprentice gardener, knew W. J. Stables and became friendly with him.

The reason 'Tinkerbell' still survives is due to the modern miracle of micropropagation. Ed Pickin of Telford, Shropshire, a keen grower of shows, took in 1980 what was believed to be the last remaining plant to Dr Roger Westcott, who was involved in tissue culture research at Birmingham University. Dr Westcott first experimented with an alpine variety, 'Vulcan', then successfully propagated 'Tinkerbell'. All the plants now in circulation stem from this early experiment. To the best of our knowledge no other green raised before 1945 still exists, but this statement is made with caution as it is not unusual for plants thought extinct to reappear. A few plants raised by Cyril Haysom, the leading grower and hybridizer of the 1940s and 1950s, are still grown but are collectors' items and not viable show plants.

The most influential raisers of greens since 1945 were Cyril Haysom, who was employed as Manager by G. H. Dalrymple at the Bartley Nurseries Southampton, Dr Robert Newton of Cheadle Hulme, Cheshire and Fred Buckley of Macclesfield.

On retirement Haysom continued to raise auriculas at Totton in the New Forest and many of his plants bear the names of villages in that area. Dr Newton and Buckley were both active in the 1950s and 1960s. Finally, David Hadfield of Cheadle Hulme raised many fine varieties in the 1970s and 1980s and is the leading hybridizer of greens at the present time. 'Prague' and 'Jupiter', both leading greens, are typical of his seedlings. Other growers have contributed on a smaller scale; another leading variety, 'Fleminghouse', attributed to J. Stant, was raised from seed given to him by Dr Newton. Of Newton's plants, 'Roberto' appears regularly on the show bench, while only 'Chloë' and 'Superb' of Buckley's many fine seedlings are still shown regularly, although not to the high standard of earlier years.

Following Haysom the influence of Dr Newton was considerable and for a time many of his plants, such as 'Greensleeves', 'Christopher', 'David' and 'John' were pre-eminent. Unfortunately, after his sudden death in 1968, they rapidly faded away and only 'Roberto', which made a remarkable comeback, is now considered a leading variety. There has been a reluctance among some of today's growers to use Newton's plants for hybridizing due to his habit of crossing grey with green. 'Roberto' ('John' x 'Teem') is a good example: raisers' lack of enthusiasm is due to the probability of producing 'china edged' greens.

Fred Buckley of Macclesfield was a superb grower, whose standards and meticulous attention to detail were unique. We knew Robert Newton, but Buckley was not as approachable and in his later years withdrew into semi-isolation. When he was nearly eighty he sent some of his plants to several leading growers. Harold Hall of Woburn Green, near Milton Keynes, was one whom we knew. Harold related how a parcel arrived quite unexpectedly containing several of Buckley's seedlings including 'Chloë', for many years afterwards the premier green. Stories abound that illustrate the dedication and single-minded approach of Fred Buckley. When his collection was distributed it was noticed by some recipients that the clay long tom pots, in which he grew his plants, had enlarged drainage holes. This had obviously been done in a most careful manner while the crocks, pieces of broken pot that cover the drainage hole in the bottom of the pots, had been shaped to make a perfect fit.

The modern greens therefore have a comparatively narrow lineage and this may be one reason why some find them difficult to flower to an acceptable standard, yet the quality and vigour are superior in many respects to the earlier plants, except for 'Tinkerbell'. This variety, a capricious plant, was always scarce and appearances on the show bench were rare despite its high reputation. We refer to 'Tinkerbell's' quality rather than vigour because it was considered a difficult variety to grow. Tom Meek of Stillingfleet, the legendary editor of the Northern Society yearbook who wrote under the pseudonym of 'Teem', once described 'Tinkerbell' as having a 'sparse, mean appearance and if one of the lower leaves is lost, it looks lop-sided for months'.

List of Varieties

We refer to the 'Midland and West Top Sixes' when describing some varieties. The 'Midland and West' Section have operated a voting system, started by Jack Ballard when he was editor of the yearbook, for over thirty years. A number of experienced growers, from all three Sections, vote for the best plants they have seen, not just at shows, during the current year. The results are collated and published in the form of tables with comments in the yearbook. The groups are separated as follows; green edged, grey edged, yellow self, selfs excluding yellow, gold-centre Alpines, light-centre Alpines and double auriculas. The Top Sixes will be referred to, in following chapters, when describing both Alpines and doubles.

Chloë (F. Buckley, 1957). For many years the premier green, it was a sensation on its first appearance at London in 1969. 'Chloë' raised the standard for greens and has since won many premier awards. A stately plant whose best feature is a beautiful, well-proportioned golden tube with no serrations. I remember seeing it at the show for the first time (writes Peter Ward) and can clearly recall the occasion. Later I went to see it again in the company of Dr Duthie, who was the exhibitor.

To our surprise and his shock it had disappeared but a moment later Mr W. R. Hecker appeared, introduced himself to Duthie, then explained that the plant had been removed to a side room to be photographed for his forthcoming book *Auriculas and Primroses*. It is still well worth growing but vigour has deteriorated and 'Chloë' has become difficult. This was Buckley's favourite, which he named after his wife. Still ranked fifth in the Midland and West Top Sixes in 1992.

Dr Duthie (P. Ward, 1975, 'Fleminghouse' x 'Chloë') An example of how disappointing a seedling can prove to be. On its first appearance at Solihull it was given an Award of Merit. Since then it has won two premier awards but is a poor grower and usually has only three or four pips, on some of which the petals do not overlap properly.

Emerald (F. Buckley, 1962) One of Buckley's less acclaimed seedlings that has occasionally performed well on the show bench. It is a darker green, still grown but quite rare. This may be one of those plants that are succinctly described by Dr D. A. Duthie of Newcastle-under-Lyme, a great authority on the auricula, as 'one good truss every five years'.

Figaro (D. Hadfield, 1985, 'Chloë' x 'Haffner') David's latest named seedling and one for which he has high expectations. It rivals 'Prague' in vigour and the variable pips, at their best, show excellent form. One of the authors has it under trial but so far it does not exhibit the reliability of 'Prague'.

Fleminghouse (J. Stant, 1967) Corsar Cup, 1967. Apparently from seed supplied by Dr Newton and named after a lane in Huddersfield. In appearance, typical of Newton's greens with a smattering of meal on the petals and ragged tube; rival of 'Chloë' and considered by some Northern growers to be superior. It has won many premier awards particularly at Manchester. Although the parentage is not known it may be a green x grey cross, let down (in our view) by the tube which is inferior to that of 'Chloë'. Generally a good grower that offsets well but 'Fleminghouse' has never flowered as well in the south of England as it does in the north. Placed second in the 1992 Midland and West Top Sixes and consistently highly placed in previous years.

Gretna Green (F. Buckley) Another Buckley seedling that has been shown successfully on several occasions. A darker green that can be classified as a 'second string' variety.

Gruener Veltliner (R. Taylor, 1992, 'Orb' x 'Hew Dalrymple') A new variety that was Premier, although a small plant with only three pips, at the 1992 Manchester show. A well-proportioned flower with considerable promise but we have yet to see if it has staying power. This cross produced a large quantity of seed; this also happened on at least one occasion when David Hadfield crossed 'Hew Dalrymple'. The unusual name is due to Bob Taylor's penchant for naming his plants after anything that comes in green bottles!

Haffner (D. Hadfield, 1974, Fleminghouse x) Corsar Cup, 1980. Another of David Hadfield's seedlings that grows quite well but has not proved a consistent performer on the show bench. It again is a darker green.

Hew Dalrymple (C. Haysom, 1947) Considered by many to be Haysom's best green although this is probably due to its superior stamina, which has enabled it to be grown to the present day. Used for crossing by David Hadfield and, as already noted, the pollen parent of 'Gruener Veltliner'.

Jack Wood (D. Hadfield, 1983, Fleminghouse x) Corsar Cup, 1983. Another fine Hadfield green that is still very scarce. I have been given this variety twice but to my frustration both plants just faded away. David has no record of the pollen parent and considers this plant to be lacking in reliability.

John (R. Newton, 1962) Considered one of Newton's better plants with a light green edge but typical large irregular tube. It almost disappeared from circulation but has been revived by tissue culture. While this form of propagation has succeeded in producing healthier looking specimens of several older plants, good flowering trusses have been harder to produce.

Julia (L. Rollason, 1976, 'Chloë' x 'Geldersome Green 2nd') A seedling from Midland grower Les Rollason. It seems a good grower and a fine plant was shown by Brian Coop of Cambridge at the 1992 Midland show. The growth habit looked to be excellent but as it has been around for almost twenty years, with little previous success on the show bench, appears to lack reliability.

Jupiter (D. Hadfield, 1976, 'Fleminghouse x') A very fine plant on its day, that was awarded two Premiers in 1992. A fresh, bright green with good proportions but a poor grower for most people. It has an unfortunate tendency to over-offset, producing a weak crown. Apart from the raiser few have succeeded with it so far but despite this it has been in the Midland and West Top Sixes for the last five years.

Orb (D. A. Duthie, 1970, 'James Stockhill' x 'Bisterne') An erratic performer that at its best can produce nice round pips of an unusual olive green shade. The tube is round but serrated and inclined to be over-large.

Paris (D. Hadfield, 1978, 'Fleminghouse x') Corsar Cup, 1978. Another from David for which he originally had high expectations. This didn't live up to early promise; it did not flower with any regularity and David has discarded it.

Prague (D. Hadfield, 1976, 'Chloë' x 'Fleminghouse') Corsar Cup, 1976. A fine plant derided by some but we think the Premier green now. A strong healthy grower that regularly produces a large flower truss. Not perhaps the finest of pips, which do vary from plant to plant, but the combination of good flowering performance with excellent growth habit gives it our vote. Voted first in the Midland and West Top Sixes three times in the last four years.

Roberto (R. Newton, 1969, 'John' x 'Teem') Newton's best green and a plant that has made a major comeback. After Newton's death it seemed to fade away but has returned to win Premier awards and is now considered a leading plant. At its best a fine show plant with beautiful flat round pips of a lighter shade of green. In its youth shown with ten or more pips but a good specimen will now carry six or seven at most. Apart from 1990, a regular in the Midland and West Top Sixes over the past ten years.

Serenity (J. Ballard, 1957, 'Haysom seed') To our amazement this variety is still grown by quite a few people. Its only virtue, when raised in 1957, was that it flowered every year which most other greens did not. Not highly regarded even then by its raiser, it has a poor pip, petals noticeably pointed.

Superb (F. Buckley, 1962) Regarded by David Hadfield very highly; not as reliable as 'Chloë' but a combination of neat tube, deep-black body colour, and better edge make it worthy of consideration.

Tinkerbell (C. Cookson, 1932) From the immediate post-War years until the late 1960s this plant was considered superior to all other greens. Invariably when 'Tinkerbell' appeared on the show bench it was awarded Premier, but such appearances were infrequent. A difficult plant to grow well, it was revived, as described earlier, when the last remaining plant was tissue cultured. Some quite good specimens have been seen in recent years leading at least one well known expert to say he considered it superior to 'Chloë'. 'Tinkerbell' was awarded Premier at the 1985 Midland show, a micropropagated plant exhibited by Ed Pickin, but apart from this has had little other success since returning to the show bench, in common with most of these revitalised plants.

Zoë (D. Hadfield, 1976, 'Chloë' x 'Fleminghouse') Corsar Cup, 1982. The same batch of seed that produced 'Prague' also gave 'Zoë'. Always rare but on one occasion we have seen it, shown by David, we think superior to 'Prague'. Unfortunately not nearly as good
a grower, flowering erratically, and it has remained scarce.

GREY-EDGED

The main difference between grey- and green-edged auriculas is the coating of meal on the petals and leaves of the former. In some varieties, Buckley's 'Grey Dawn' for example, the leaves are without meal but this is quite rare. Dr Newton once wrote that the grey-edged auricula represented the quintessence of the auricula's charms, something with which we entirely agree. The density of the meal varies from a light sprinkling, giving a grey-green effect, to a heavy covering when the edges become almost white. In some varieties the edge of the flower is outlined with a distinct margin of silver. The combination of silver edge, grey and white of the paste, with the black body colour, produces a colour scheme of stunning beauty that is unique. The mealed foliage can be heavily serrated and is particularly attractive when this is so. "I remember," says Peter Ward, "many years ago, seeing Jack Ballard's plants in his greenhouse at Droitwich. Jack, a former President and editor of the yearbook of the Midland Section, was particularly keen that his plants should look good even when not in flower. He did this by feeding although he always

denied doing so. As he was telling me this I noticed two large tins of fertilizer on the shelf under the greenhouse staging. At the time there were about 1,000 plants in the greenhouse of which a large number were grey-edges, mostly seedlings. They were all much larger than normal and the luxuriant heavily mealed foliage, most with serrated leaves, was a magnificent sight even though the trusses were still in bud."

The pips of grey-edged varieties are usually smaller than those of the green-edge. The more heavily mealed the pip the smaller it tends to be and lightly mealed varieties like 'Warwick' can have much larger pips. Where the pips are very heavily mealed the plant is classed as a white-edge but true white-edges are rare and several varieties have appeared at shows in both classes. Therefore we are not inclined to describe the white-edge as a distinct group although the shows of the National Auricula and Primula Society still have separate classes.

In parallel with the greens Haysom was by far the most influential post-1945 raiser of greys, and his dominance was even greater in this section. He raised many varieties and most of the modern plants are descended from his strain. Although some Haysom greys still exist they have deteriorated and have been surpassed by the newer plants. One that remains a force, with which he was not originally identified, is 'Teem', introduced by Thomas Meek of Stillingfleet. Speculation concerning the parentage of 'Teem' has been considerable but it is now generally accepted that it was raised from Haysom seed, the source for this information being Dr Newton. The other outstanding grey of the 1960s and 1970s was 'Jessica', given to Dr Newton by Haysom as an unflowered seedling. These two plants dominated during the period and were never seriously challenged by any other variety.

Both Newton and Buckley, the other outstanding raisers at that time, produced grey-edged and white-edged seedlings. From Buckley came 'Elegance', 'Grace', 'Grey Friar', 'Helena', 'Grey Dawn', and 'The Bride' that has been shown both in the grey-edged and white-edged classes. 'Grey Friar' and 'Helena', although not outstanding, are a different type of grey with no similarity to the Haysom varieties. 'Grace' was very good on its first flowering but in the following seven years didn't bloom. It is assumed that Buckley used other parents for his strain although he also grew many of Haysom's plants. His family had a long tradition of growing auriculas, an uncle is pictured in a group photograph of Northern growers in 1895. He inherited a collection of plants, after being given his first auricula at the age of twelve by his father, which included many older varieties. Not all Buckley's seedlings were successful, an all-too-familiar pattern with show auricula hybridizers.

Dr Newton's greys and grey/whites lacked real quality although he has frequently been described as the raiser of 'Jessica', something that he never claimed, stating quite clearly it came from Haysom. Two of his greys, 'Sea Fret' and 'Hathor', obtained at least one Premier but faded away. Another that he rated highly was 'Grey Seal', generally considered a white-edge, still grown but much inferior to the better varieties of the last few years.

In recent years several other good greys have been raised. This upsurge began in 1974 when the late Arthur Martin of Droitwich exhibited a 'Lovebird' x 'Teem' seedling at the Midland show. It was given an immediate Award of Merit and received another at the Manchester show the following week when it was named 'Margaret Martin' after his wife. The maiden plant was of stunning beauty and while several Premiers have been awarded to other plants of 'Margaret Martin' since, none have attained the standard of the original.

The use of 'Teem' as a pollen parent was taken up by other raisers and from Ron Cole of Messingham came 'St Boswells' awarded one excellent Premier but frequently let down by a poor tube. Peter Ward began an intensive breeding programme producing 'Warwick', 'Gavin Ward', and 'Sharmans Cross' in 1976, 'Brookfield' in 1979 and 'Clare' in 1980. All except 'Sharmans Cross' have gained Premier awards, several in the case of 'Warwick' and 'Clare'.

Most recently David Hadfield has shown 'Grey Hawk' and 'Iago' where a different line of breeding was followed; the intention was to produce a true grey rather than the grey/whites where 'Teem' is the pollinator. The introduction of these plants is very recent but 'Grey Hawk' has already been awarded two Premiers.

List of Varieties

Almondsbury (J. Stant, 1973) A moderate grey of unknown parentage that was found in a box of seedlings given by Jack Stant to another Northern grower. Of reasonable form and initially considered quite good but has not fulfilled early promise.

Brookfield (P. Ward, 1979, 'Walhampton' x 'Teem F2') A vigorous if somewhat untidy grower with one Premier award. Best feature a nice round tube with no serrations. A good beginner's plant that can be grey or white, but not in the top rank.

Clare (P. Ward, 1980, 'Walhampton' x 'Helena') A vigorous grower and reliable flowerer. Quality is variable, a comment that applies to most edged auriculas; at its best can be very good and already has several Premier awards. In the Midland and West Top Sixes for the last six years.

Dorothy Midgley (J. W. Midgley, 1945)

Corsar Cup, 1946. J. W. Midgley was a leading figure in the Northern society and judged the show section for many years. 'Dorothy Midgley', named after his daughter, was the best white-edge of its time, which is now long past. At least one Premier award, and is still being used as a parent.

Elegance (F. Buckley, pre-1968) A 'second string' Buckley plant that appeared on the show bench for a short period. A reasonable grey/white but not in the top rank.

Gavin Ward (P. Ward, 1976, 'Walhampton' x 'Teem') A very fine grey that is named after Peter Ward's son. Considered by him to be his best grey and very close to Glenny's 4-2-1 formula. While a good reliable grower it is still rare as offsets are not freely produced. At least one Premier award and despite its scarcity has appeared in the Midland and West Top Sixes since 1983, missing only in 1987.

George Rudd (T. Woodhead, 1882) A famous plant that as late as 1963 was first and third in the single grey class at the Midland show. More has been written about 'George Rudd' than almost any other auricula and it has been the source of much mythology. Haysom called it 'a so-called good auricula', while Dr Newton described Rudd as 'a roughish flower that grows like a weed'. It remains in cultivation after more than 100 years, following micropropagation.

Grey Friar (F. Buckley, 1968) Buckley's best grey, a good grower and a well regarded plant that is being used for hybridizing. A true grey but unfortunately the pips do not flatten properly, creating a rather corrugated effect. This lets it down which is unfortunate as the tube, paste, and body colour are excellent.

Grey Hawk (D. Hadfield, 1988, 'Hawkwood' x 'Unnamed Fancy') A new grey with two Premiers already in its short career. David Hadfield has been attempting to breed true

greys rather than the whitish grey 'Teem' progeny that predominate; described by show judge Allan Guest rather well as 'a real grey with a leaden look'. A rather dull tube has attracted some criticism; there is also a question mark regarding vigour. David has used 'Grey Hawk' as a parent but the progeny, while of high quality, also show this disturbing lack of vigour.

Grey Tarquin (T. Newton, 1982, 'Fleminghouse' x 'Elegance') A green x grey cross that first flowered in 1984. The tube, paste and body colour are almost identical with those of 'Fleminghouse', with the edge similar to 'Elegance'. Due to its late flowering habit show appearances so far have been rare, but well thought of by such a good judge as David Hadfield.

Helena (F. Buckley, 1968) Of a similar type to 'Grey Friar' and possibly from the same parentage. A less refined flower with a heavy body colour that can flash out almost to the edge. Awarded two Premiers; the most recent at Saltford in 1990.

Iago (D. Hadfield, 1988, 'Grey Friar' x 'Stephen') A plant of similar type to 'Grey Hawk', but not rated as highly by David Hadfield although some other good judges consider he is being over-critical. 'Stephen', the pollen parent, was raised by J. Stant; a plant of quality but rarely seen on the show bench. Voted fifth in the 1992 Midland and West Top Sixes.

James Arnot (T. Meek, 1961, 'Gloria' x 'J. W. Midgley') A white-edged variety often spoilt by a large misshapen tube. Nevertheless considered one of the better whites and won the Corsar Cup for best seedling at Manchester in 1961. It had faded away over the last few years but made a strong comeback in 1992 when several very good examples were shown by Ike Hawthorn of Newbury. James Arnot was a Scots grower and friend of Tom

Meek.

Jessica (C. G. Haysom, 1954) Of unknown parentage given to Dr Newton by Haysom amongst a batch of unflowered seedlings. Considered by most experts to be the best grey of its day although variable and not the strongest of growers. It has always been scarce but still got seven Premier awards, including one in the mid-1980s in London. Most of the Premiers were plants with three pips, occasionally five. A beautiful if fragile plant.

Lovebird (J. Douglas, 1935) A Bookham nursery plant that was the leading grey for a few years in the 1950s. During this period it was awarded at least two Premiers. A variable plant that, to quote Dr Newton, 'can be grown to show standard but only now and then'. Two clones were said to exist, one of which had a smaller, more refined, tube. This variety still survives today and has been micropropagated. Not comparable with modern varieties; a curiosity for collectors just like 'George Rudd'. Notable as the seed parent of 'Margaret Martin'.

Ludlow (E. Pickin, '1985 Embley' x 'Teem') Another 'Teem' seedling that won the Corsar Cup for best seedling at Manchester in 1986. So far it has not lived up to this early promise, proving a poor grower. The seed parent 'Embley' was a little-known Haysom variety.

Margaret Martin (A. Martin, 1973, 'Lovebird' x 'Teem') A sensational plant on its debut at the 1974 Midland show. Given an Award of Merit at this and the following Manchester show, where it also won the Corsar Cup for best seedling. Several Premiers to its credit but the quality of the maiden plant has never been equalled. Can be described as a more refined version of 'Lovebird' but it does have faults such as a narrow body colour, which is incomplete in places and a crenated tube. First or second in the Midland and West Top Sixes five times in the last eight years.

Minstrel (L. Wright, 1986, 'Douglas Seed') A typical 'Douglas' plant with excellent tube and paste. It is a real white and appears to have potential as a parent. Some years ago Dr Duthie visited Gordon Douglas and selected two near-white seedlings in bloom that he subsequently called 4X and $3\frac{1}{2}$X. He noticed that the Douglas strain, while deficient in some respects, had small round tubes and good dense pastes. The tubes were better than those on most of the named grey/whites and these two seedlings, never named, were passed out to several raisers who have used them for hybridizing.

Orlando (D. Hadfield, 1988, 'Grey Friar' x 'Stephen') The same cross as 'Iago' and considered by David to be the better plant. It has the desired 'leaden look' and bears some resemblance to its pollen parent.

Rosalie Edwards (H. Hall, 1969) This was given to then Midland Society Treasurer, Dennis Edwards, by Harold Hall. Dennis named it after his daughter and in 1970 at Birmingham and Manchester 'Rosalie' created great interest. For a time it was a most sought-after auricula but didn't live up to early promise. A good tube and striking, truly black body colour are the main attributes.

Sharmans Cross (P. Ward, 1976, 'Walhampton' x 'Teem') A seedling that took several years to settle down which is now an acceptable show plant; more often shown as a white. Not as good as 'Warwick' or 'Gavin Ward'; all from the same cross. A typical 'Teem' seedling.

St Boswells (R. Cole, 1972, 'Sea Fret' x 'Teem') Awarded Premier at the 1976 Manchester show. Another 'Teem' seedling that flattered to deceive. Although it has won several prizes it didn't live up to early promise. Variable and mainly let down by its large tube. On occasion it has been shown with a smaller tube, in which form it is a fine plant but vigour is poor.

Teem (T. Meek, 1957, 'Haysom seed') Won the Corsar cup on its debut at Manchester and dominated the grey class, with 'Jessica', up to the late 1970s. After seeming to fade away has returned to winning form in recent years, gaining the Premier for Bob Taylor at Manchester in 1989. Renowned as an excellent pollinator, its progeny dominate the grey class. 'Teem' should have won many more Premiers but suffered from the tendency of judges to give the award to a green-edged plant. Apart from 1987–8 has been in the Midland and West Top Sixes for many years and placed fourth in 1992.

The Bride (F. Buckley, 1959) Described by Dr Duthie, when grown by Buckley, as 'the best white I have ever seen'. Often more grey than white and disqualified on one occasion when shown in the white class as 'not according to schedule'. A good round tube is set off by a brilliant deep-black body colour, contrasting well with the grey/white edge. The pips tend to be few and good specimens have been rare in recent years.

Walthampton (C. G. Haysom, pre-1960) One of Haysom's later introductions that never became widely distributed. A good white at its best but success on the show bench was shortlived. Famous as the seed parent of 'Gavin Ward', 'Warwick' and 'Sharmans Cross'.

Warwick (P. Ward, 1976, 'Walhampton' x 'Teem') One of the best greys with several Premiers. An improvement on its parent 'Teem', with strong similarities. It took several years to settle down but had quality from the beginning. Although a reasonable grower it tends to shrink in winter and has the annoying habit of producing offsets high up in the leaf axil. First or second eight times in the Midland and West Top Sixes in the last ten years.

THE SELFS

Selfs are show auriculas whose flowers are uniformly coloured from the paste to the margin. As the term 'self' was once used to describe alpine auriculas their history remains unclear, but it is thought that they date from the early part of the nineteenth century.

The very wide range of colours set off so vividly against the white paste attracts many people, more so perhaps than the edged varieties. The colours range from a very pale yellow-green through red and purple to an intense black.

The selfs flower earlier than the edged varieties and due to their thinner petals have a much shorter blooming period. They are generally easier to flower and most produce a larger number of pips than the edged plants. Similar criteria are used to judge them except, of course, they have no edging. Roundness of petal, flatness of pip, and even colouring (shading being considered a serious fault) are paid particular attention.

Selfs were comparatively rare in the immediate post-1945 period but gradually, as interest increased, the number of new seedlings has proliferated and they are now more numerous than edged plants. One reason for this is that it is easier to breed new varieties; nor are they so perverse, being generally more reliable in their flowering performance. Considerable interest exists in extending the colour range, with a variety of mainly paler shades appearing at present-day shows. The main problems with these new seedlings are that they are frequently deficient in form, or when form is satisfactory the colour shaded.

We have already seen that the outstanding raisers of edged auriculas during the early modern period were Haysom, Newton and Buckley. The position is nothing like as clear-cut with selfs, although all made contributions, mainly in the yellows.

YELLOW SELFS

The yellow selfs are much admired and the most numerous of the different colour forms. They are also closest to *P. auricula*, in fact a highly refined development of what is thought to be one of the original parents of show auriculas. In common with many other selfs thin petals are prevalent and slight notching of the petals is another fault in many varieties.

From Cyril Haysom came 'Ower' and 'Melody', the parents of many modern varieties. 'Ower', raised in 1938, was the leading yellow self for a long period. 'Melody', raised two years earlier, came to the fore rather later and was Premier at Birmingham in 1969, a rare honour for a self. Dr Duthie has told how he exhibited, as a novice grower, an 'Ower' at Manchester that was awarded the Premier. This caused some comment from some of the older growers and the subsequent yearbook listed 'Dorothy Midgley', a white-edged plant, as Premier!

Dr Newton produced three yellows: 'Streamlet', 'Isis' and 'Leeside Yellow'. 'Streamlet' had fleeting success but 'Leeside Yellow', a rather poor grower, has done better due to its later flowering habit.

From Buckley we had 'Yellowhammer', 'Goldilocks', and 'Queen of Sheba'. These plants have meal-free foliage and Dr Duthie, who purchased Buckley's plants in 1969, thought the parentage to be 'Willowbrook' x 'Bookham Star'. 'Willowbrook' ('Edith Winn' x 'Harrison Weir') was raised pre-1940 by Tom Sheppard, and 'Bookham Star' even earlier, in 1918, by James Douglas.

In the 1970s a variety called 'Sunflower', origin unknown, achieved success although considered a 'rough variety' by Jack Ballard and some other experts. The other contender was the controversial 'Sheila' from Allan Hawkes: a frequent winner but heavily criticized by some of the older growers who did not like the way the colour faded.

The two outstanding yellows of the early 1980s, still highly ranked today, were 'Brompton' from David Hadfield and 'Tracy Ward' from Peter Ward, both 'Goldilocks' x 'Melody'. They were joined by 'Upton Belle', from the late Dick Rossiter, that was actually raised a few years earlier but took longer to establish.

Now many high-quality yellows are appearing from several raisers, notably Tim Coop of Harrogate, many of whose plants are paler shades, for example 'April Moon' and 'Sherbert Lemon'. Les Kaye of Sheffield won the Corsar Cup in 1988 with 'Golden Fleece', a rich-yellow seedling with excellent form, while Ken Bowser of York exhibited a lovely 'Brompton' x 'Upton Belle' seedling at Cheadle in 1991.

In the South of England Lawrence Wigley has worked on yellows since 1976, when he raised several hundred seedlings from six specific crosses, each involving 'Melody' as pollen parent, except for one cross which was 'Melody' x 'Chorister'. From these some thirteen plants have been named and given the 'Beeches' prefix, many of which have won prizes at London shows. As yet they have made little impression further North.

Over the next few years the current leading varieties may be eclipsed, such is the momentum underway in raising new plants in this class.

List of Varieties

April Moon (T. Coop, 1988, 'Moonglow' x 'Helen') A beautiful, vigorous new self with large pips of excellent form. A paler yellow than 'Tracy Ward' or 'Brompton' but a fine plant that, if it maintains early promise, will be a leading variety. Has featured in the Midland and West Top Sixes in four of the last five years.

Beeches Excellence (L. E. Wigley, 1976, 'Sheila' x 'Melody') With 'Beeches Polonaise' and 'Beeches Jan' considered by Lawrence his leading three. A rich golden yellow with good petal texture and excellent form; a good paste and tube with a strong flower stem. A tough stocky plant with moderately mealed foliage that offsets slowly.

Beeches Jan (L. E. Wigley, 1976, 'Seedling' x 'Melody') Generally nearer to 'Melody' with creamy yellow flowers, excellent paste, tube and petal texture. Foliage is moderately mealed; grows well but offsets slowly and has inherited 'Melody's' fault of short footstalks.

Beeches Polonaise (L. E. Wigley, 1976, 'Melody' x 'Chorister') A good bright yellow with a well-arranged head of flowers. The tube, paste and petal edge are excellent. A strong grower with moderately mealed foliage that offsets freely.

Brompton (D. Hadfield, 1978, 'Goldilocks' x 'Melody') A fine plant, the leading variety now with its combination of good form, rich colour and consistency. The individual pips are spaced well apart on a tall stem and the only criticisms are a tendency for the blooms to reflex, while the anthers project slightly out of the tube. 'Brompton' is a good grower and offsets freely. Voted first or second in the Midland and West Top Sixes for the last nine years.

Corntime (T. Coop, 1988, 'Moonglow' x 'Helen') Another from Tim Coop, a rather paler shade.

Elsinore (P. Ward, 1976, 'Yellowhammer' x 'Sunflower') A good grower and offsetter with lightly mealed, large rounded leaves. The colour is a rich yellow and the pip is reasonable but has a hint of unevenness around the edges. The tube and paste are acceptable but could be better. A good beginner's plant. Now dropping out of the Midland and West Top Sixes after a good run.

Goldenhill (D. A. Duthie, 1971, 'Willowbrook' x 'Sunflower') From the same cross as 'Guinea', a slow-growing plant that offsets infrequently and is a poor flowerer. Very heavily mealed leaves and a bright, richly coloured, pip make this an attractive plant when it decides to perform. Very scarce and may now be extinct.

Goldilocks (F. Buckley, 1958) An almost identical plant to 'Queen of Sheba' and may share the same parentage. Notable mainly for the meal-free leaves as the flowers are not outstanding. A good rich colour but the pips are thin in texture and the paste is on the narrow side.

Guinea (D. A. Duthie, 1971, 'Willowbrook' x 'Sunflower') The twin of 'Goldenhill' but of entirely different character. 'Guinea' is a vigorous grower, offsets freely and is a reliable flowerer. Although a good colour the pips display several faults. A beginner's plant lacking real quality.

Harvest Moon (L. Rollason, 1976, 'Rosebud' x 'Sunflower F2') A good reliable grower with neat, lightly mealed foliage. The pips are of medium size, pale-yellow and variable in form. Another beginner's plant.

Helen (T. Coop, 1981, 'Douglas Old Gold Seedling' x 'Chorister') A vigorous and easy variety that multiplies rapidly. Many pips of reasonable quality are produced that need thinning out. 'Helen' is proving an excellent parent.

Leeside Yellow (R. Newton, 1965, 'Melody' x 'Ower') Newton's best yellow although a weak grower that rarely put up more than five pips; in recent years three are more common. Resembles its pollen parent, 'Ower', in appearance but less robust with large medium-yellow pips of a somewhat thin texture. Its success is as much due to the late flowering habit when many other yellows are finished. Not up to the standard of the modern varieties.

Lemon Drop (T. Coop, 1984, 'Moonglow' x 'Helen') A lemon-coloured self that is proving very reliable. It produces small neat pips on a large well-formed truss, although the paste is on the narrow side. Not as good as 'April Moon' and 'Sherbet Lemon', but it is a vigorous grower that rapidly makes a large plant.

Melody (C. G. Haysom, 1936) The pollen parent of 'Brompton' and 'Tracy Ward' that in its day was one of the best two yellows, the other being 'Ower'. Premier at Birmingham in 1969, a rare honour for a self; always scarce and in the shadow of 'Ower' but kept going when 'Ower' began to fade. Still surviving but is now very rare and difficult to keep.

Ower (C. G. Haysom, 1938) For many years the Premier yellow; a fine plant that was also micropropagated by Dr Roger Westcott. The resulting plants flowered well for several years afterwards but vigour has again declined. Used extensively as a parent by many hybridizers, mostly with disappointing results; it is, however, the pollen parent of 'Moonglow'.

Party Time (T. Coop, 1984, 'Moonglow' x 'Helen') A small plant with well-mealed leaves, this seedling is not as vigorous as the others. It is again a paler yellow with good form.

Pot o' Gold (G. Baker, 1975, 'Chorister' x 'Sunflower') Neat foliage with a yellow tinge to the meal inherited from 'Chorister'. The tube and paste are acceptable on the medium-sized rich-yellow pips. A good grower producing offsets too freely, to the detriment of flowering.

Queen of Sheba (F. Buckley, pre-1966) Very similar plant to 'Goldilocks' and might be from the same cross.

Sheila (A. Hawkes, 1966, 'Douglas Seed') A controversial plant criticized by the older fraternity for its colour, that tends to fade. Nevertheless took the first three places in the yellow self class at London in 1972. 'Sheila' has now been superseded by the newer varieties.

Sherbert Lemon (T. Coop, 1984, 'Moonglow' x 'Helen') A beautiful pale-yellow with a satiny texture to the petals. It is a sturdy long-lived plant that is proving rather shy in producing offsets. There has been slight controversy over the colour shade, probably misplaced, with some growers feeling it should be shown as 'any other colour'. The quality is such, however, that 'Sherbet Lemon' could challenge any of the present top varieties in the next few years. Entered the Midland and West Top Sixes in 1991 in third place and maintained this position in 1992.

Tomboy (T. Coop, 1984, 'Moonglow' x 'Helen') This has the advantage of flowering later than the other seedlings from the 'Moonglow' x 'Helen' cross so may still be in flower for the later shows. The form is reasonable with a pip that flattens well, but the paste is hexagonal.

Tracy Ward (P. Ward, 1976, 'Goldilocks' x 'Melody') A lovely plant that can produce a beautiful rounded truss with flat, well-formed pips of a rich texture and colour. For a period it looked like becoming the unquestioned leader in its class but has become unreliable. Grows well with heavily mealed leaves but is rather slow at producing offsets.

Upton Belle (R. G. Rossiter, 1974, 'Sunflower' x 'Chorister') Premier at Knowle in 1992. When introduced it seemed to lack vigour. It is due to the perseverance and skill of Ed Pickin that 'Upton Belle' has prospered. Now considered one of the finest yellows because of the sumptuous beauty of the large pips. Form is not quite as good as either

'Tracy Ward' or 'Brompton' but petal texture is superior. The foliage has a distinctive appearance with narrow leaves, slightly serrated, that are lightly covered in meal. Voted first or second in the Midland and West Top Sixes in four of the last five years.

Willowbrook (T. Sheppard, pre-1945, 'Edith Winn' x 'Harrison Weir') Another older plant considered very good in its day and used by raisers to breed new varieties. Still in existence although very rare and not comparable with the modern seedlings.

Yellowhammer (F. Buckley, pre-1968) An unusual yellow from Buckley of quite a different type being a very large vigorous plant with lightly mealed foliage. The pips are large and richly coloured but often few in number. Most growers suffered with cockled pips but Hal Cohen, past President and doyen of the Midland Section, showed two magnificent specimens in 1978 with absolutely flat pips and in this form it was unbeatable. Unfortunately this has never been repeated and 'Yellowhammer' has since faded away.

RED SELFS

Good red selfs have never been numerous and 'Harrison Weir', raised in 1908 by James Douglas, was supreme until the beginning of the 1970s. A few other varieties were grown including 'Fanny Meerbeck', raised by Ben Simonite in 1898, and 'Adonis' by Sam Barlow in 1883. Both 'Harrison Weir' and 'Fanny Meerbeck' still survive but 'Adonis' is probably extinct. 'Alice Haysom' was raised by Cyril Haysom in 1935; it also survives, so we can see that red selfs are in general long-lived.

The rise of the modern reds started with the introduction of 'Cherry' and 'Redgauntlet' in 1968, and 'Pat' in 1969. 'Pat', raised by Jack Ballard, was given an Award of Merit at Birmingham. 'Adonis' was the pollen par-

ent and the colour, a bright red, was an advance on the existing varieties. Dr Duthie showed 'Cherry' at London, where it was awarded a first; and 'Redgauntlet' at the Manchester show the following Saturday. 'Redgauntlet' was also awarded first prize and the Corsar cup for best seedling. 'Harrison Weir' was the seed parent of 'Cherry' but the pollen parent in both cases was an interesting little plant known as 'HMR1'. This stood for 'Hall Mikado x Rosalind'; the plant one of a large batch of seedlings that Harold Hall produced from this cross. Harold gave away most of them and Dr Duthie was one such recipient. He noticed that one seedling, although a dark-red, had very good form. Tried as a seed parent no success was achieved but as a pollinator some excellent seedlings resulted. The main problem was a tendency to transmit the darker colour as well as good form. Dr Duthie subsequently passed plants of 'HMR1' to, among others, Peter Ward who used it to produce his 'Indian reds', 'Geronimo', 'Cheyenne', and later 'Kiowa'.

The prime requirement in breeding new red seedlings, given as much priority as form, is brighter colour. Trevor Newton of Stockton on Tees has taken things a stage further using 'Pat', 'Cheyenne', 'Redgauntlet' and lesser known plants like 'Red Cardinal', to produce 'Red Sonata', 'Red Embers', 'Red Vulgan' and 'Ring O'Bells'; all very promising new varieties with bright colouring but still to prove themselves.

List of Varieties

Alice Haysom (C. G. Haysom, 1935) Described by Hecker as 'a bright cardinal red' but, in comparison to the latest seedlings, of very dark colouring. A good tube and reasonable proportions were offset by a coarse paste. This is another variety that remained scarce and was exhibited infrequently.

Alfred Niblett (H. A. Cohen, 1963, 'Haysom Seed') Described by Ed Pickin, who has a keen eye, as a 'dusky red' with small neat pips of five or six petals. By the mid 1970s superseded by 'Pat' and the 'HMR1' offspring.

Cherry (D. A. Duthie, 1968, 'HMR1' x 'Harrison Weir') On its debut, at London in 1968, this cerise red self caused a considerable stir and is the plant that is pictured in W. R. Hecker's 1971 book, also published by Batsford, *Auriculas and Primroses*. Despite a promising beginning 'Cherry' did not make a major impact though winning many prizes, particularly at Northern shows. The colour appeared to deteriorate, becoming more maroon with a bluish cast, and it shared 'Red-gauntlet's' habit of over-offsetting, leading to a weak crown. Both these seedlings inherited the yellow tinged foliage of 'HMR1'.

Cheyenne (P. Ward, 1971, 'Pat' x 'HMR1') 'Cheyenne', with 'Geronimo', have been the leading reds for the last fifteen years. Form is excellent with good tube and paste, but the colour is now regarded as on the dark side. This is due to the effect of 'HMR1'; both are brighter than their pollen parent but slightly darker than 'Pat'. The foliage is not terribly attractive, again taking after 'HMR1', being very lightly mealed, the meal prone to a yellowish tinge in late autumn and winter. The other fault, from the exhibitor's point of view, is the early flowering habit that causes many good specimens to miss the shows. A regular in the Midland and West Top Sixes, 'Selfs other than Yellow', and the highest-placed red self over the last fifteen years.

Geronimo (P. Ward, 1971, 'Pat' x 'HMR1') Originally Peter Ward considered 'Geronimo' to be better than 'Cheyenne' but they have become so similar that, in practice, they could be the same plant. Although not making large plants both grow well and offset freely.

Harrison Weir (J. Douglas, 1908) A very famous auricula that was only superseded in the early 1970s. Raised at Edenside by James Douglas, the nursery that was also renowned for carnations. 'Harrison Weir', after whom the plant was named, was a well-known practical horticulturist, as well as animal painter and author; also a designer and engraver on wood. To quote the famous 'Teem', writing in the 1956 Northern yearbook, 'This variety will have gained more awards than any other self and in 1950 at Birmingham was shown in such remarkable form that it was awarded the premier card'.

When Buckley's collection was purchased by Dr Duthie in 1971 and plants from it subsequently distributed, Peter Ward obtained 'Harrison Weir'. He subsequently showed two plants that were described by an experienced grower as 'the best examples he had seen for years'. 'This surprised me', writes Peter, 'as they did not seem to me to be very special at all, and certainly not nearly up to the standard of 'Cheyenne' and 'Geronimo'.' This illustrates, we believe, the improvement in quality that has taken place in the last thirty years.

Kiowa (P. Ward, 1976, 'Pat' x 'HMR1' x 'Pat') 'Kiowa' was intended to replace 'Cheyenne' and 'Geronimo'; a plant with brighter colouring and better foliage. The colour is excellent: a very bright colour verging on orange-red. The foliage is also better being heavily mealed without the undesirable yellow tinge. In other respects it has proved deficient, the form more comparable to 'Pat', with a pip that has an uneven or ragged outer rim on both the paste and edge. Another problem, again inherited from 'Pat', is the small number of pips on the truss.

Pat (J. Ballard, 1966, 'Pimadel' x 'Adonis') 'Pimadel' was one of Jack's earlier seedlings, a 'pinkish colour', while 'Adonis' was a famous auricula raised in 1883 by Sam Barlow. I have to add that some well-known growers have expressed doubts that the plant grown at this time was the true 'Adonis'. Misnaming of auriculas is not uncommon with quite a few impostors masquerading under famous names.

'Pat' received an Award of Merit, a rare occurrence, at Birmingham in 1969 and for a time was the leading variety. Still competitive today, the foliage is heavily mealed, the pip displaying a slight unevenness around the outer edge of the paste. Form is not as good as 'Cheyenne' and recently 'Pat' has become less reliable: it is difficult to get more than four pips. As a parent 'Pat' has been quite successful and is still being used for crossing by hybridizers.

Redgauntlet (D. A. Duthie, 1968, 'Will Eckersley seedling' x 'HMR1') 'Redgauntlet' caused a considerable stir when first shown, winning the red class and Corsar Cup for best seedling at Manchester in 1969. It was considered superior to 'Cherry', with large bright-scarlet pips that could be of excellent form. Later, in Duthie's words, 'the feet of clay were noticed' when it produced double crowns and offsets at an alarming rate. Although good specimens have since appeared they have been rare, with the other damning fault that the pips will rarely flatten and are usually cockled.

Red Beret (D. Telford, 1980) This is a very bright-red seedling with small heavily-mealed, almost white foliage. The leaves are pointed with no serrations. Form is moderate and the plant is not a strong grower, tending to over-offset leading to a weak crown.

Red Cardinal (S. Kos, *c.* 1971, 'Melody' x 'Alice Haysom') This is a little-known plant; the raiser was Stan Kos, a member of the Northern Section in the early 1970s. He wrote a number of articles for the yearbook

describing his attempts to raise new varieties, mostly green edged. We understand that the cross was 'Melody' (the well-known Haysom yellow) x 'Alice Haysom'. 'Red Cardinal' is an unusual shade of red, leading several growers to use it for hybridizing. The foliage is moderately mealed and distinctive but the flower stem is short, so that the truss does not fully clear the foliage.

Red Sonata (T. Newton, 1989, 'Red Cardinal' x 'S8A seedling') A small neat plant with well-mealed pointed leaves; a lovely bright-red with good form. Trevor has been line breeding red selfs and 'S8A' is an unnamed seedling with parentage of 'Headdress' x 'Redgauntlet' x 'Cheyenne'. 'Headdress' is one of Derek Telford's earlier reds. If this seedling maintains its early form it will become a leading variety.

DARK SELFS

Although a popular class, the number of dark selfs is relatively few and the class has been dominated by three varieties, 'Mikado', 'Neat and Tidy' and 'Barbarella'. 'Mikado', raised in 1906, is still going strong and is a fascinating plant, reigning supreme until the 1960s. 'Neat and Tidy', raised by Dr Newton from Haysom seed, was prominent from the early 1960s until quite recently, although 'Mikado' was never superseded; a plant with considerably more quality and character. Derek Telford raised 'Gizabroon' and 'Blackhill', both 'Neat and Tidy' seedlings, that have appeared regularly on the show bench. 'Barbarella', a 'Mikado' seedling, appeared from Peter Ward in 1980 and has become very popular. More recently we have had 'Erjon' in 1990 and 'Old Vinovian' in 1992 from Trevor Newton; these may be the plants of the future.

List of Varieties

Barbarella (P. Ward, 1980, 'Pat' x 'Rosalind' x 'Mikado') A vigorous plant that bears a strong resemblance to 'Mikado' although the leaves are lightly covered in meal. An excellent grower that offsets freely and produces, at its best, a large truss of well-formed black pips. On some specimens the pips can be dark red but the combination of vigour and reliable flowering make it the leading dark self. Voted first in the Midland and West Top Sixes, 'Selfs other than Yellows', four times in the last five years.

Erjon (T. Newton, 1987, 'Mikado' x 'Black-hill') A very fine, new dark self that created a great impression when shown at Cheadle Hulme in 1990. The pips were large of excellent form, lustrous black with a slight blue sheen. The following year, while good, the pips were smaller and the blue sheen was missing. Nevertheless an excellent new variety of great promise. 'Erjon' is named after one of Trevor's dogs.

Gizabroon (D. Telford, 1974) A darkish red with a brown cast that has well-mealed foliage and a large truss of medium-sized pips. Derek originates from the North East and the name reflects the colloquial Geordie way of asking for a glass of Newcastle Brown Ale! 'Gizabroon' is not one of the best dark selfs, but as they are few has done well on the show bench.

Mikado (W. Smith, 1906) 'A very fine dark self; shown in all my first prize groups. First in its class 1907–8; F.C.C., National Auricula Society 1906, A.M., R.V.S., 1906.' This quotation was attributed to James Douglas of Edenside in 1913. Properly known as 'The Mikado', this amazing plant is now nearly ninety years old yet continues to be shown in excellent form. 'Mikado' is a most distinctive auricula and is easily recognized by the foliage. The leaves are long and lanky, without meal, and tend to flop over the sides of the pot. They are light green with a touch of yellow; they are serrated at the edges. The truss is carried on a tall stem producing an adequate number of pips. At their best the pips are large, sumptuous and black. In its other form more pips are produced but are smaller and a very dark red.

Some years ago 'Mikado' became very scarce and was thought to be on the verge of extinction. Stock was reintroduced from Scotland while Harold Hall of Woburn Sands began producing particularly fine large specimens from which he distributed many offsets. When asked how he did it, Harold replied that he gave 'Mikado' no special treatment: "It just grows like that!"

Later 'Mikado' received another boost when the Buckley plants were distributed by Dr Duthie. Buckley had, besides his seedlings, many well-known established varieties. The difference was that his 'clones' seemed superior in all-round vigour, perhaps as a result of his meticulous attention to every aspect of cultivation. One such plant was 'Mikado', where the 'Buckley clone', as it became known, was a far superior plant to the one grown by others. Although unquestionably the same variety his plants have a slight sprinkling of meal down the midrib of the leaf that led some growers to question if it is in fact the true plant.

Neat and Tidy (R. Newton, 1955, 'Haysom seed') From the early 1960s to the mid-1980s 'Neat and Tidy' was one of the best dark selfs. It is now less often seen but at its peak was a vigorous and prolific variety that produced a large truss of dark-red pips. From the same batch of seed Dr Newton grew the very similar 'Nocturne', a less vigorous plant thought by some growers to be superior. Dr Duthie summed it up as a 'weak Neat and Tidy'.

Old Vinovian (T. Newton, 1991, 'Erjon' x

'Barbarella') The latest from Trevor that won the seedling class at Cheadle in 1992. Initial impressions are of a plant with excellent form, good dark colour and very flat pips.

BLUE SELFS

The desire to raise a pure-blue self has always been a cherished wish of auricula hybridizers. It is generally felt, from what we know about the pigmentation of auriculas, that this is unlikely. Nevertheless hybridizers continue to try and some nice flowers of a 'horticultural blue', that is a more violet shade, have been produced. They are rare and the problem of impure colour remains, together with other criticisms that include pale tubes and weak constitution. A further annoying fault common to blues is that petaloid stamens can occur in the pips.

The original blue self was 'Mrs Potts', said to be the plant illustrated in colour in the 1948/49 yearbook of the Northern Section. The plant shown is purple and is described as such.

The modern blues are mostly related to 'Blue Fire' raised by James Douglas in the early years of this century. This plant still exists and Brian Coop has one that last flowered nine years ago! For many years it was the only blue self available until the early 1950s when Clive Cookson, of 'Tinkerbell' fame, sent the Rev. Oscar Moreton of Bloxham in Oxfordshire some blue seedlings. An offset, described on the label as 'C2-Blue Seedling Self from 'Bluebird'', was passed on to Dr C. D. Hough. He exhibited it in a six at Manchester in 1956 where it was named 'Bloxham Blue' and given an Award of Merit. Most subsequent blue crosses involved 'Bloxham Blue', 'Blue Fire' and other seedlings from Cookson's original batch, some of which were also sent to W. R. Hecker. Dr Newton raised 'Blue Nile' and 'Stella',

while 'Remus' and 'Renata' came from Hecker. The Rev. Moreton produced 'Throckmorton' and 'Gladys Moreton' in the early 1960s but neither were distributed before expiring. 'Over Worton' also came from Bloxham in 1959 and was still around until quite recently, used by Dr Duthie in his blue crosses. None of these plants had staying power and most have disappeared.

Until recently the only modern varieties of note were 'Blue Jean' and 'Oakes Blue' raised by Derek Telford of Oakes, Huddersfield. Both were from a 'Stella' x 'Everest Blue' cross and 'Oakes Blue' is considered the best blue, though a variable plant with many traits associated with this colour type.

Finally, in 1991 Trevor Newton exhibited several excellent seedlings at Cheadle Hulme, creating much interest. These plants were from a cross between a 'Stella' x 'Nathan Silver' seedling and 'Moonglow'. The surprising parent was 'Moonglow', which is a very pale lemon self, slightly shaded around the tube. The colours of these seedlings vary from purple to a clear light blue and form is excellent. The light blue seedling was the winner of the Corsar Cup and has been named 'Prince Bishops'. It is still very early to make a judgement in view of the unpredictable behaviour of auricula seedlings.

List of Varieties

Ann Hill (C. F. Hill, 1958, 'Blue Fire' x 'Fearless') 'Fearless' was a violet/purple Douglas variety with attractive foliage but no real quality. The attractive foliage was passed on to 'Ann Hill' which can put up a large truss of many pips of moderate form. This has always been a scarce plant, producing few offsets that are slow to mature.

Blue Jean (D. L. Telford, 1972, 'Stella' x 'Everest Blue') 'Blue Jean' differs from most blue selfs in having long, narrow, green leaves on which a very light sprinkling of meal appears in spring. It produces a moderate truss of small pips with a good even colour.

Blue Nile (R. Newton, 1962, 'Blue Fire' x 'Bloxham Blue') A good blue in its early years and considered an easier one to manage. Stock builds up quickly although adult plants are difficult to maintain.

Everest Blue (H. D. Hall, 1959, 'Haysom seed') Another interesting plant that has faded away in recent years. Of different appearance to 'Blue Fire' and its progeny the foliage is lightly mealed with leaves that curl downward. A good sized truss with large pips of a blue/violet colour is set off by a tall flower stem. Harold raised this plant from seed obtained from Cyril Haysom. When first exhibited as a seedling at London Haysom asked him how he had raised it. According to Harold, Haysom looked very surprised when he was told it was from his seed.

Nathan Silver (E. Green, 1965, 'Everest Blue' x 'Blue Fire') This is another rare plant that has never become widely available. 'Nathan Silver' has short wide leaves, lightly mealed and slightly serrated. The pips are large with a round tube but the edge of the paste is uneven.

Oakes Blue (D. Telford, 1972, 'Stella' x 'Everest Blue') This is the best blue self and has been voted in the first three, 'Selfs other than Yellow', of the Midland and West Top Sixes for the last seven years — the first blue ever to feature. It is a small- to medium-sized plant with narrow, well-mealed leaves. The pip is medium-sized and is the nearest to true blue we have, although on many occasions can appear slightly shaded. Form is quite good with a nice round tube and wide paste of good texture, although slightly uneven on the outer edge.

Prince Bishops (T. Newton, 1990, 'S4B seedling' x 'Moonglow') 'S4B' is a 'Stella' x 'Nathan Silver' cross. This is the plant that created great interest at the 1991 Cheadle show when it won the Corsar Cup. The colour is a light pure blue, more so than any other variety so far, and the tube looked yellowish rather than the usual pale insipid shade. This may have been due to the anthers that had lovely yellow pollen, again rather unusual in blues. The name is that of a family of hereditary landowners in the north-east. Others to look for from this cross are 'Blue Merle', 'Smart Tar' and 'Valerie June'. The colours of these other seedlings vary and are not as good as 'Prince Bishops'. We shall have to see if 'Prince Bishops' has the stamina to match its undoubted quality.

Remus (W. R. Hecker, 1970, 'Cookson seedling' x 'Blue Fire') In 1953 W. R. Hecker received some blue self seedlings from Clive Cookson. They were presumably from the same batch that were sent to Rev. Moreton. After crossing and recrossing them for several generations 'Remus' was produced, 'Blue Fire' having been introduced at the third generation. Although considered good on its introduction our verdict is that this is another over-rated plant without much to commend it. 'Remus' has dark-blue pips that frequently appear shaded and the growth habit is very poor due to over-offsetting.

Renata (W. R. Hecker, 1970, 'Cookson seedling' x 'Douglas seedling') A much superior grower to 'Remus', with long dentate leaves that have a light covering of meal. At its best, not seen in recent years, a tall stem supported a large head of pips of a dark violet/blue, again showing signs of shading.

Stella (R. Newton, 1965, 'Bloxham Blue seedling') When first introduced 'Stella' was very similar in colour and form to 'Bloxham Blue'. It suffered from similar defects, the principle one being a miserable growth habit with weak crown surrounded by a collar of offsets. On occasion it can be very good but has rarely appeared at the shows. Due to its colour hybridizers have used it extensively.

OTHER SELFS

While the selfs already described represent the principle categories some plants do not fit into these colour groups.

James Douglas raised some selfs whose colours were variously described as red-bronze, maize, old-gold, mid-pink, and rose-pink. Other colours crop up from time to time in seedling crosses but the main problem is that they do not usually conform to standards in two respects: the form is often deficient while colours are impure and frequently shaded.

Nevertheless, a few plants have become established, for example 'Isabel' from Dr Newton, which is a heather purple. Another striking plant is 'Moonglow' from David Hadfield, a very pale lemon that many people find delightful. Others disagree, pointing out the slight shading around the tube. 'Moonglow' has created enormous interest in recent years with some outstanding progeny in blue and purple from Trevor Newton, and many shades of yellow from Tim Coop. Brian Coop produced 'Blue Steel' from Douglas seed, a unique colour although not up to exhibition standard, without the violet purple shade prevalent on the other blue selfs. This plant has been crossed with a wide range of non-standard colours, and the raiser is confident that new colours will appear as a result. Considerable effort is being made at present to extend the colour range and the next few years should see many new seedlings introduced.

List of varieties

Isabel (R. Newton, 1962, 'Bloxham Blue' x 'Blue Fire') Corsar Cup, 1965. Of the seedlings kept from this cross 'Isabel' was the least blue, being a heather- or reddish-purple. Now very rare it has longish narrow leaves that are well-mealed. The pips are medium-sized and of reasonable form with a slightly narrow paste. On occasion it has been shown with a dozen or so pips, in which form the appearance was striking.

Lilac Domino (A. Delbridge) From a 'failed' blue cross this is a small, neat, lilac-purple plant with few faults. It is not different enough for some growers but is a regular winner.

Limelight (T. Coop, 1988, 'Moonglow' x 'Moneymoon') This is a pale-greenish cream, a shade lighter than 'Moonglow'. A small plant with lightly mealed leaves that is an improvement on its seed parent. At the moment it is not proving over-vigorous and is still very scarce. This variety has been voted into the Midland and West Top Sixes in the last two years.

Moonglow (D. Hadfield, 1975, 'Leeside Yellow' x 'Ower') First shown by its raiser at the 1976 Manchester show. Former President Frank Jacques subsequently recorded in the Northern yearbook: 'Mr Hadfield delighted everyone with a creamy-green seedling that he named 'Moonglow', an appropriate description for this gem of a flower.' The colour is aptly described but the petals are on the thin side, tending to give an impression of slight shading around the tube. Nevertheless a beautiful plant that has given the 'any other colour' class a considerable boost. It is easy to grow and offsets well. 'Moonglow' is also producing some splendid offspring in a variety of unusual shades. Since its introduction a regular in the 'Selfs other than Yellow' section of the Midland and West Top Sixes.

FANCIES

In *Auriculas and Primroses*, W. R. Hecker stated that the group of auriculas known as the fancies had never been clearly defined. He went on to say that any auricula of the show type that does not conform strictly to the accepted standards might be called a fancy. More than twenty years after this was written little has changed other than the re-introduction of striped auriculas as a separate group. It has been suggested that flowers with body colours other than black be defined as fancies but there is no reason at all why such plants, providing they conform to the accepted standards in other respects, should not be considered edged varieties. Fancies therefore may be classified as plants that do not conform to the basic standards but are sufficiently striking to make them worth retaining. The tube and paste should be of an acceptable standard but the remainder of the flower judged for effect.

List of Varieties

Coffee A grey with a *café au lait* body colour raised by Gwen Baker from a 'Love-bird' x 'Teem' cross.

Conservative Acquired by David Hadfield at a Northern plant sale in the early 1970s this is a red ground, grey edge that can on occasion give the impression of being striped. It has been assumed that it came from the Douglas nursery. It is an interesting fact that the colour adopted by the Conservative party in the North of England was usually red, whereas in the South it is blue.

Error One of the better known of the modern fancies from Allan Guest, a small grey with a purple body colour. As is common with these plants, the pip is on the small side and is often lacking in edge.

Green Isle A green edge with a red body colour that has been winning prizes recently.

Hawkwood An old Douglas plant, grey with a dark-red body colour that has been a reliable variety for many years. This one is possibly the nearest to normal show standards which is why David Hadfield has used it for hybridizing. Unfortunately it is not a reliable grower and this trait has manifested itself in its offspring.

Helen Mary A green edge with a purple body colour that made a good initial impression. It was subsequently micropropogated but has not lived up to initial promise. The pips are small and lacking edge with too much body colour.

Rajah Another Douglas plant, bright scarlet body with green edge, popular for over twenty years. Compared to the standard greys and greens with black body colour it is very rough.

Rolts/Rolts Fancy A green edge with a red body colour that is a regular prize winner; sometimes called 'Rolt's Green'.

Spring Meadows A green edge with a yellow body and one of the most popular fancies. While in no way conforming to show standards many consider the flower very pretty. Raised by Jack Ballard who was always looking for something different.

Sweet Pastures Raised in 1957 by Jack Ballard and still a popular variety; green edged with a delicate yellow body colour.

Star Wars and Space Age Two from Tim Coop of Harrogate who crossed a pin-eyed, purple-bodied seedling obtained from Allan Guest with another grey edge. From this cross many greys with different body colours were produced although many were pin-eyed. Tim has made further crosses with these seedlings and some interesting plants are beginning to appear.

STRIPED

Some three hundred and fifty years ago striped auriculas were much sought after and this popularity continued until the latter half of the eighteenth century. Many illustrations survive, both watercolour drawings and pressed flowers, in some well-known museums and libraries such as the Queen's Library at Windsor Castle, and the Victoria and Albert Museum.

For unexplained reasons, probably the cycle of ever-changing fashions, the stripes disappeared and this remained the position until the early 1960s. We should mention that Sir Rowland Biffen, who died in 1949 shortly before the publication of his classic work, *The Auricula*, had tried to recreate striped auriculas and illustrates one such seedling there. In 1965 Allan Hawkes, perhaps inspired by Biffen, decided to attempt their recreation beginning with a green edge seedling that showed a slight tendency towards striping. This was a plant given to Allan by Dr Cecil Jones of Llanelli, better known as a raiser of double primroses. After many years of crossing and recrossing, using a mixed bag of plants, slowly but surely seedlings began to appear with the desired striping. The initial plants were poor in quality but a steady improvement has taken place with earlier varieties being rapidly superseded. Even now the tube, paste and roundness of the pip of most of these striped seedlings does not approach the standard of the other show varieties; plants are also on the small side. Allan Hawkes is confident that these faults will be eradicated with further breeding and selection but some feel the ragged outline may be more difficult to eliminate.

Inspired by Allan's example other growers are breeding stripes, notably Allan Guest of Rochdale. He started with pollen from Allan's plants in 1983, crossing it on to one of his own seedlings, 'Error,' a white-edged show with a blue body, and a mauve ground Douglas fancy named 'Frank'.

List of Varieties

April Tiger (A. Hawkes, 1985, 'Tiger Bay' x 'seedling') This is a vigorous and consistent seedling with mauve stripes on a grey-white ground colour. Some offsets have already been distributed.

Arundel (R. Downard, 1986, 'Pin eyed striped seedling' x 'Rajah') Freely available due to its habit of producing large numbers of offsets, sometimes at the expense of a flowering truss. A most interesting plant with green and red-brown stripes on a grey ground.

Blackpool Rock (A. Guest, 1988, 'Error' x 'Singer Stripe') A plant prone to 'rotting off', it is pink with white stripes. The unique blend of colours is accompanied by a less-than-smooth outline. Described by Allan as 'the most unusual and the most difficult of the batch'.

Konigin der Nacht (A. Guest, 1988, 'Error' x 'Singer Stripe') Opera lovers will recognize the name as that of the Queen of the Night from Mozart's *Magic Flute*. Described by Allan as 'a delectable lady, displaying her colour now as a dark-purple rather than black, though her stripes remain white'. A vigorous plant, with beautiful white leaves, that is prone to rotting off.

May Tiger (A. Hawkes, 1986, 'Rover Stripe' x 'Conservative') The colour varies slightly but is usually greyish stripes on a dark-red ground colour. This plant has apparently been micropropogated and should be available fairly readily.

Mrs Davies (A. Guest, 1988, 'Error' x 'Singer Stripe') Considered by Allan to be the best of these seedlings and named after his mother. The blooms are a rich purple shade with white stripes but the pips vary considerably in quality. 'Mrs Davies' is a relatively good grower but slow to offset; the leaves are finely mealed.

Raleigh Stripe (1979, seedling cross) This is one of the earlier stripes, most of which Allan named after 'antique' bicycles, another of his many interests. It was one of the best of the earlier seedlings and has survived partly due to a striking colour combination of red stripes on a yellow-buff ground.

Rover Stripe (A. Hawkes, 1975) An earlier stripe raised by Allan Hawkes from a striped seedling cross. At the time it represented a significant advance in quality over previous seedlings and is still worth growing. Colour is dark-red stripes on a greyish ground; the paste is reasonable. This variety has been micro-propogated and is available commercially.

This concludes the various types of show auricula. We have given brief details of a selection of the better varieties. There are many others not mentioned that are or may still be grown. Some are old varieties that are difficult to maintain and rarely flower. A greater number are seedlings, of mainly moderate or poor quality, named by their raisers and distributed perhaps unwisely. In addition many promising seedlings appear annually and it is possible that we have overlooked some that will become well known in the years ahead.

3 Alpine Auriculas

Alpine auriculas are the simplest Florists' auriculas, more numerous, easier to obtain and grow than show auriculas. This makes them ideal plants for the new grower, suitable material for learning how to grow auriculas, before progressing to the slightly more difficult and expensive show auriculas. They have no connection with alpines or rock plants other than name, but it is easy to get the two confused, so it is normal to write the name with a capital to clarify matters. Like all auriculas other than borders, they are the work of enthusiasts, produced by hand-pollinated seed from pedigree parents. Their chief characteristics are that the flowers are shaded, the colours being deepest next to the eye, becoming progressively and uniformly lighter in colour, with the lightest shade adjacent to the outside edge. As with all Florists' auriculas this edge is as circular as possible. The whole plant is completely devoid of farina, on leaves, stalks and flowers and the majority offset readily.

Alpine auriculas first rose to prominence in the last century. There is some record of shaded plants being developed in the U.K. in the first half of the nineteenth century, two of the most prominent being 'King of the Alps' and 'Queen of the Alps'. They became popular in the latter years of the Victorian era: new varieties were introduced by a nurseryman called Charles Turner at the Royal Nurseries, Slough and the House of Douglas, prominent in auricula circles until the death of Gordon Douglas, a grandson of the founder, a few years ago. A few of the old Douglas varieties are still with us, winning prizes on the show bench, while the oldest auricula known is an Alpine auricula called 'Argus', which our records show was first exhibited in 1890, well over one hundred years ago. Such is its vigour and perfection of form that after more than a century of vegetative propagation, 'Argus' is still winning prizes on the show bench and yet will as soon form a large clump in gardens.

Many people ask if these Alpine auriculas are suitable for growing in the garden. This depends on the variety – many are, but some have not the stamina to withstand heat, frost, pests and other hazards. They were selected for their perfection of form and suitability for display rather than garden decoration and endurance. They are formal plants, selected to fit an exacting specification and are rather stiff, prim and proper with their pattern of concentric rings, so their presence will depend on the garden and the gardener's taste. In addition, they have only a short flowering period and so are not suitable for bedding purposes. The related polyanthus are much more suitable due to their longer flowering period. Many varieties do well outside and form big clumps but some do not have the stamina that borders have, making them more suitable for planting in the garden.

Alpine auriculas are usually grown in pots in a cold frame or greenhouse until they have flowered. This keeps the beauty of the flowers in pristine condition, protected from being dashed by wind or rain. For show purposes they are normally kept to a single crown, similar to show auriculas; the schedules only allow one truss, though for other purposes such as general greenhouse display they can be grown in clusters in larger pots. The number of flowers developing varies from one variety to another. A truss of twenty-two fully open flowers is not unknown, but nine to eleven is about the maximum that can be successfully borne; the minimum allowed in exhibiting is five. There also seems to be an optimum size to the pips; over-large flowers tend to magnify faults, to lose that indefinable grace and poise, and are condemned as 'blowsy'.

In Alpine auriculas even the slightest trace of farina is considered a fault, particularly on the flowers. Despite this stricture some well-considered older varieties ('Verdi' is the most famous example) do have traces of farina on the flowers. The colour of the petals shades from the deepest in the centre, next to the eye of the pip, fading uniformly to a lighter shade at the edge. This shading is considered an important part of their beauty, allied to perfection of form. Both the tube and the outside edges of the flowers should be as

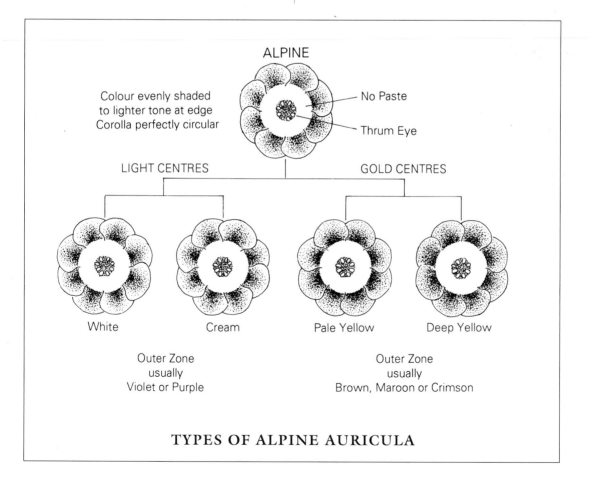

ALPINE

Colour evenly shaded
to lighter tone at edge
Corolla perfectly circular

No Paste

Thrum Eye

LIGHT CENTRES   GOLD CENTRES

White   Cream   Pale Yellow   Deep Yellow

Outer Zone
usually
Violet or Purple

Outer Zone
usually
Brown, Maroon or Crimson

TYPES OF ALPINE AURICULA

circular as possible, without nicks or serrations on the petals. The grading from the edge to the centre should be balanced and in proportion. Sometimes the inner circle or 'eye' becomes angular, spoiling the effect and this is more prevalent with five or six petals. The number of petals may be as many as eight but this number should be constant in all the pips on a truss. Often the petals overlap slightly; it is considered most desirable if they overlap consistently, either right to left or vice versa, except where the petals come full circle. There is usually one petal with both edges exposed and perhaps one with both edges obscured by other petals. The limb of the petals should be flat, as both 'cupping' and 'reflexing' are regarded as detracting from the beauty of the plant and are considered faults. The centres or 'eye' can be of two colours, either a bright clear golden yellow, when the plants are known as gold-centred Alpines, or it may be white or a light-cream colour, known as light-centred Alpines. Of late some attractively shaded varieties, with primrose centres once described as the colour of 'cold custard', have been introduced. Initially they were frowned on by the judges and considered inferior to the clear colours of the other varieties. These 'custard centres' seem to be the result of crossing gold centres with light centres, something that purists deplore. An old variety from the House of Douglas, 'Prince John', also has this type of centre, which it tends to pass on to its seedlings. These plants are usually considered gold centres, though not so meritorious as the recognized types.

There is a large number of named varieties of Alpines: many are very similar in colour and difficult to tell apart. At least three shows a year (in the U.K.) have a new seedlings class, for both gold and light centres. The top three winners can be named, so eighteen new varieties may arrive annually. This rarely happens as the number and quality vary from year to year, but in poor years seedlings may be named that really ought to be discarded. In general there is a large number of good or average plants, and a few that produce an exceedingly fine truss on occasion, for instance 'Quality Chase'. Finally, there are the best, reliable varieties, such as 'Sandra' which has had three Premier awards in recent years.

Over the years the number of petals in the flower has increased from the original five, to between six and seven or exceptionally eight. This has been accompanied by an increase in size and substance and has helped with the attempt to produce a circular centre on the flower. Varieties, or sometimes plants with one pip and only five petals, tend to have a pentagonal centre, spoiling the symmetry of the flower and so the truss. Depending on the level of nutrition of the plant, later-opening flowers on the truss may have fewer petals. In addition the tube may become slightly deformed, being elliptical rather than round, and the juncture between the colour of the tube and that of the petals angular or slightly ragged. Both of these are faults and while this does not matter much in the garden or greenhouse, such flowers are not good enough to exhibit. Alpine auriculas are a beautiful sight when displayed *en masse*, even more beautiful than a single plant, with their rich velvety texture, delicate shading and wide range of colour. All the society flower shows have separate sections for Alpines and separate classes for the two types, gold centres and light centres. While good displays of Alpines are normal at the spring shows of the auricula societies, one particular Northern show a few years ago had an exceptionally large number of plants on display. On that occasion there were several hundred gold and light centres and the beauty of the display was breathtaking, 'a glittering array of jewels'.

GOLD CENTRES

The pigments of the two original parents, yellow flavin and pink/red/mauve hirsutin are combined in gold centres. As these pigments are found in different layers of cells many beautifully coloured flowers are found. The flowers have a rich, deep velvety texture, as one colour is viewed through the other. The golden tube, the centre of the flower, shows some slight variation in both colour and roundness; the most circular and the deepest gold are preferred. The shaded part of the flower still retains this yellow ground colour and various concentrations of red or brown pigment occur in the outside part of the petals, shining through the gold. Some striking colour combinations have resulted and the class can be divided into red gold centres, like 'Winnifrid', and brown gold centres, like 'Rodeo', differing slightly from one variety to another. In general the shaded flowers are deep crimson, bright scarlet, cinnamon brown, or golden brown, with all shades in between, from the deep crimson, near-black of 'Galen' and 'Kim', through the crimson of 'Blossom' and 'Winnifrid', to the spice and marmalade colours of 'Rodeo' and 'Merridale'.

LIGHT CENTRES

The light centres have a softer beauty than the gold centres, as they lack the yellow pigment, flavin, inherited from *P. auricula*. Their shading and colour usually display pinks, mauves and purples, depending on the concentration of the hirsutin present and the acidity of the sap, losing the brilliance of the underlying gold. High concentrations of the pigment give flowers an intense deep purple like 'Rabley Heath', or a deep velvety red like 'Joy', both of which were favourites some fifteen to twenty years ago. 'Joy' is a variety where the colour is too deep to show much shading and this has become less acceptable compared to plants where it is more pronounced. The majority of varieties, however, are paler and softer shades of pink, mauve and purple. In this section the nearest we have to a true blue auricula is perhaps 'Mrs Walton', often grown only for its colour, rare in auriculas. Another variety of near-blue colouring is 'Ann Taylor', raised by Bob Taylor of Keighley, Yorkshire. One of the most popular is 'Mark', a brilliant pink and very vigorous; a photograph exists of 'Mark' growing in the open garden. To some eyes such Alpines look too artificial for this setting; the unsophisticated borders fit the bill much better, though this is a matter of personal preference.

In the last few years there has been a new colour break, led by the 'custard-centred' 'Sirius', a chance seedling produced by the late, well-known Northern grower and judge, Frank Jacques. The story is told that he thought it poor and threw it on the compost heap, the usual fate of failed seedlings. However, his wife Jean was so attracted by the unusual brown and yellow shading that she made him rescue it. The plant was subsequently shown at Cheadle and created a great stir as another variety whose uncommon colour compensated for a slightly imperfect form. 'Sirius' has since been used as a parent, producing a range of seedlings with outstandingly attractive colours. They include 'Lee Paul', 'Dusky Maiden' and 'Sir John' – all with better form than their parent and much in demand.

While relatively few raisers have dominated the introduction of new varieties of show auriculas since 1945, this is not the case with Alpines. Prior to the Second World War the House of Douglas had been the dominant commercial source, raising a large number of varieties several of which are still with us today.

When this famous nursery closed in 1967, Gordon Douglas, the grandson of the founder, continued to grow auriculas in a large greenhouse he built in his garden. He also exhibited at the Chelsea Flower Show and until three years before his death in 1988 was still selling plants and seed. The plants were mainly seedlings and he did not introduce any notable new varieties during this period, although some fine plants, of which 'Blossom' is the best known, have been raised from his seed.

The most important raiser in the 1950s and 1960s was Frank Faulkner who came from an auricula-growing family. Frank had been familiar with auriculas since the beginning of the century and had begun hybridizing using a gold-centred seedling called 'Tom Jones' raised by his father. In 1951 he introduced 'Frank Faulkner', named after his father, which was described by both Dr Newton and Dan Bamford as the best gold centre raised this century. A whole series of new varieties, including some light centres, came from his greenhouse at Morecombe over the next twenty years. 'Forge' was considered his best seedling by some, others preferred 'Peter Faulkner', while 'Winnifrid' was possibly the most successful on the show bench.

C. F. Hill of Birmingham was another major raiser and details of his hybridizing are given in Chapter 7. He introduced 'stable' names, as most of his raisings were given names ending in 'o', 'Bolero' and 'Rodeo' for example. On his death his friend and auricula 'partner' Allan Hawkes, of Rabley Heath, maintained this line of breeding. Fred had asked Allan to continue with his 'o' names, which he did in all cases where Hill plants were directly involved. He also wanted a gold centre named after him, so Allan changed the name of the best seedling he had at the time from 'Scorpio' to 'C. F. Hill'. Allan does not confine his breeding to Alpines and has produced some doubles as well as bringing back striped auriculas.

Many other people have raised good seedlings, sometimes only one, for instance the gold centre 'Blossom' raised by Mrs S. E. Auker from Douglas seed. This was another very influential plant, a leading show variety and successful parent. Two of its better-known seedlings are 'Sandwood Bay' and 'Applecross' raised by Dennis Edwards from Jack Ballard's seed. 'Blossom', although thought to lack vigour in its earlier years, remains competitive and has won Premier awards recently.

Jack Ballard was responsible for several good Alpines, chiefly gold centres. 'Quality Chase', 'Sandwood Bay' and 'Applecross' are the best-known.

More recently we have had the light centres 'John Wayne' from Frank Bailey and 'Sandra' from Hal Cohen. 'Sandra' has already won three Premier awards, while 'John Wayne', after a rocky start when it proved difficult to multiply, is becoming established as a top variety. Cliff Timpson has recently raised a nice seedling from open pollinated seed of 'Quality Chase', rather similar to its parent.

Other hybridizers of note are Arthur Delbridge and Les Kaye, both of whom have raised several very good seedlings. First and foremost, however, is Derek Telford of Huddersfield who has concentrated on Alpines, after an early dalliance with show selfs. He has raised many new seedlings including 'Jeannie Telford', named after his wife, 'Lisa' a granddaughter, and 'Lee Paul' a grandson. His best plant to date is undoubtedly the light centre 'Mark', named after another grandson, an outstanding variety which leads its class. Derek has many other seedlings coming along and is famous for giving some of them unusual names.

STANDARDS OF PERFECTION

Stem and Footstalks The stem should carry the head well above the foliage; the footstalks should be long enough and stiff enough to carry the truss well, without overcrowding of the pips. Overlong footstalks cause the pips to droop.

The Tube Should be circular and well up to the expanded pip.

The Anthers Must be well up to the level of the pip and neatly folded.

The Pistil Must not be visible above or among the anthers. 'Pin-eyed' flowers carry an automatic disqualification.

The Colour Gold, cream or white centre; body-colour cut sharp and circular where it meets the centre, shaded towards the outside edge and free from any trace of meal. The colours should be clear and rich, with no tendency to be muddy.

The Pip Round, flat and smooth, without notches in the lobes. The centre should be four-sevenths of the surface. Size and substance should be present with no suspicion of coarseness. Cupping or reflexing to be considered a fault.

The shading of the flowers of Alpine auriculas varies from one variety to another. It is considered desirable that the colour should shade evenly from the centre to the edge, as does the old light-centre variety 'Argus'. Some very attractive plants tend to shade rather abruptly from the dark in the centre to the light colour of the edge, for example the light-centre 'Frank Crosland', almost blue in colour. Other varieties that have little shading are light centre 'Joy' and gold centre 'Kim', both dark velvety crimson in colour.

The criteria for Alpine auriculas are less numerous than those for edged show auriculas; consequently many more varieties are available that meet the requirements. The following lists of varieties are not complete. A complete list would be very long indeed given the number in circulation and the quantity of new seedlings introduced annually. Included are some of the older, more notable plants, perhaps now scarce, while others are more modern, vigorous and more easily obtained. However all named varieties have generally good form and attractive colouring.

List of Gold-Centred Varieties

Alan (F. Faulkner, 1953) An excellent variety that has become scarce. The pips are shaded maroon to crimson on a short stem. In its earlier years was awarded several Premiers.

Alexandra Georgina (L. Bailey, 1980) A very scarce variety which should be better known as it possesses some quality. It produces a good truss with large pips, markedly shaded from darkest maroon to an unusual shade of light coral. Awarded a prize on its first showing as a seedling.

Andrea Julie (D. L. Telford, 1972, 'Blossom' x 'Bookham Firefly') A popular plant with large pips of a lighter shade of red than usually seen. Must be well grown to get a reasonably tall stem. A reliable, easily-grown plant that is very attractive.

Applecross (D. Edwards, 1968, 'Blossom' x 'Mrs G. Savory') Raised from seed obtained from Jack Ballard and sister plant to 'Sandwood Bay'. The pips are well shaded of a rich-crimson colour on a tall stem. This was a very popular variety for showing during the 1970s and 1980s. Jack Ballard was well known to both authors and obviously regretted giving away the seed when he saw the results.

Beckminster (G. Baker, 1989, 'Goldfinch' x 'Overdale') Red-brown shading to old gold, rather sombre, with quite large pips. From the same cross as 'Goldthorn' and 'Merridale'.

Blossom (S. E. Auker, 1970, 'Douglas seed') A rich velvety deep-crimson, shading lighter to bright red with a fine flat flower. For many years the outstanding crimson-red variety, which has also proved an excellent parent with many excellent seedlings amongst its progeny. Mrs Auker, who was known as 'Blossom' to her friends, grew this plant from seed when a novice grower. Still voted fifth in the 1992 Midland and West Top Sixes. An essential acquisition for the serious grower and hybridizer.

Bolero (C. F. Hill, 1964, 'Bratley' x 'Shako') A superb, much sought-after variety, very scarce due to its reluctance to produce offsets. Very precise medium-sized pips of copper red shaded to an unusual tone of light apricot-pink. Won a Premier award as recently as 1987 and has featured in the Midland and West Top Sixes every year since then.

Bookham Firefly (J. Douglas, 1936) There is extreme scepticism among some growers about plants circulating under this name, the suggestion being that they are impostors. Whatever the truth, the plants in circulation are of modest size, producing a large truss of small pips. The colour is a rich velvety crimson shaded lighter with an uneven bright-gold centre.

Bratley (C. G. Haysom, 1943) The raiser described this plant as having petals of a good thick texture. The colour is a rich crimson shading nicely to the edge with a fine round tube and bright gold centre. The plant has the habit of producing double crowns, a feature passed on to some of its progeny. The best trusses were produced on maiden plants. It is possible that 'Bratley' is now extinct but it has played a very important part in the pedigree of many modern varieties.

Brenda's Choice (A. Delbridge, 1987) A robust plant with large pips of a dark-purple maroon with a narrow shaded edge to the petals. The centre is a bright gold but can be pentagonal in shape.

Bright Eyes (D. Telford, 1983) A well-named plant with small pips, very dark-red shading lighter through to orange.

Cameo (C. F. Hill, 1964, 'Bratley' x 'Shako') One of the 'o' series, a small plant with medium-sized pips shading from red-brown to gold.

Dusky Maiden (A. Delbridge, 1987, 'Sirius seedling') Rather sombre colouring, brown and purple.

Eastern Queen (A. Delbridge, 1988, Open pollination 'Largo') Brown shaded to gold, gaining a Premier award as a seedling.

Erica (G. Baker, 1984, 'Prince John' x 'Winnifrid') Red, shading to rose with a rather pale-yellow centre.

Finchfield (G. Baker, 1976, 'Overdale' x 'Goldfinch') This variety can be grown into a large plant with long, wayward footstalks. The same parentage as 'Beckminster' but a much brighter gold edge.

Forge (F. Faulkner, 1957) A small plant with a short stem. Dark velvety crimson pips with perfect shading and a rich-golden tube. This plant was a favourite of the raiser and considered by some his best seedling. Not shown for some years and possibly extinct.

Frank Faulkner (F. Faulkner, 1951, 'Tom Jones' x 'Irene') An old variety that created an enormous stir when first shown as it was a breakthrough in its colouring. Both Bamford and Newton thought it the best gold centre raised this century. The stem is tall with large pips of dark crimson shading to bright, lighter red. The centre is uneven and the footstalks can be of uneven length. Despite its reputation the plant never became widely distributed and only appeared spasmodically on the show bench. The raiser named it after his father, also a famous auricula grower.

Galen (R. Cole, 1970, 'Forge' x 'Robin Hood') The large pips are of a dark, almost black, crimson with an almost complete lack of shading. Despite this it has proved a popular plant with exhibitors, perhaps because it contrasts so well when shown in a multiple class. A good easy grower that offsets well.

Gay Crusader (L. Kaye, 1982) A bright crimson with most attractive brown coloration in the outer petals. Awarded the Riddle Cup when shown as a seedling in 1982. Named after a racehorse. Voted into the Midland and West Top Sixes since 1990.

Goldthorn (G. Baker, 1976, 'Overdale' x 'Goldfinch') From the same cross that produced 'Finchfield' and 'Merridale' but has remained scarce. This is a pity as it is the better plant with large pips of very dark-red shading to a bright-gold edge. The centre is very precise.

Janie Hill (C. F. Hill, 1959, 'Bratley' x 'Tally Ho') A slow growing plant prone to forming double crowns which seems to inhibit offset production. At its best can produce a superb truss of red-brown pips that are correctly shaded to gold. A major fault can be the presence of meal in the centre.

Landy (D. Telford, 1987) The name is short for 'Orlando'. On its debut won the seedling cup at the Northern show.

Lady of the Vale (C. Timpson, 1993, 'Andrea Julie' x 'Largo') A bright-crimson new seedling, named after one of the steeples of Lichfield Cathedral.

Largo (A. Hawkes, 1969, 'Shako' x 'Verdi') A superb variety which can frequently be grown to Premier standard. The major problem is its reluctance to produce offsets while adult plants show a tendency to rot off. Apart from this it grows well with nice clean foliage

and good flowering stem supporting the most exquisite flat pips of deep-red shading to gold. This is one of the most sought after plants. Premier Alpine in 1990 at both Saltford and Knowle and voted 'best gold centre' in the Midland and West Sections Top Sixes in 1989, 1990 and 1991.

Lee Paul (D. Telford, 1990, 'Sirius' seedling) Distinctive dark-brown pips of a rather sombre shade with a gold edge that must be shown in fresh condition, otherwise ageing changes the colour. The footstalks are on the short side and can make the truss lopsided. Premiers already awarded in 1990 and 1991 and voted first in 1992 Midland and West Top Sixes. 'Lee Paul' has been successfully micropropagated and distributed in large numbers.

Lewis Telford (D. Telford, 1990, 'Blossom' seedling) Similar in colouring to its parent but with a more symmetrical flower truss.

Mahmoud (L. Kaye, 1993) Premier at Knowle in 1993 the colouring is unique, almost entirely gold except for a circle of scarlet next to the eye. The outer edge of the flower is unusually the same shade as the centre. Les Kaye names his seedlings after racehorses.

Merridale (G. Baker, 1976, 'Overdale' x 'Goldfinch') A plant whose flowering truss has long footstalks, carrying medium-sized pips with a golden orange edge, shading from cinnamon brown. It has a tendency to produce double crowns.

Mick (D. L. Telford, 1989) A very promising new variety with large brownish red pips shaded lighter, attractive colour with fine form. A winner when shown as a seedling and a possible future star.

Nic (A. Delbridge, 1990, 'Largo' seedling) Another new one from that prolific raiser and expert exhibitor Arthur Delbridge.

Nickity (C. Timpson, 1991, Open pollinated

'Sirius') A vigorous new variety with dull red pips, correctly shaded lighter.

Prince John (J. Douglas, 1916) An old yet still vigorous variety that has made a startling comeback in recent years. Excellent specimens have been shown that have been in contention for the Premier award. This is another plant where the colour changes when the pips begin to age. At its best produces a good truss of medium-sized pips of a maroon shade paling to the edge. A good seed parent. Voted second in the 1992 Midland and West Top Sixes and never lower than fifth in the previous five years.

Quality Chase (J. Ballard, 1966, 'Tally Ho' x 'Bratley') Still very scarce despite being raised nearly thirty years ago. Can be grown into a large plant but is prone to double or triple crowns with a resultant lack of offsets. The very large pips are bright brown-red shaded to gold. The large centre is variable and occasionally imprecise. This plant won a Premier in its early days then almost disappeared until reappearing to win another Premier recently.

Rodeo (C. F. Hill, 1960, 'Mrs E. Goodman' x 'Verdi') A typical 'Hill' plant with medium-sized pips, dark-red shading to burnt-orange. The petals are not always flat but the tube is neat and nicely fretted.

Sandhills (A. Delbridge, 1989, 'Sirius' seedling) Large pips of a dark-maroon shade to a lighter narrow edge of a khaki colour. A robust grower but again colour rather sombre, typical of many 'Sirius' seedlings.

Sandwood Bay (D. Edwards, 1971, 'Blossom' x 'Mrs G Savory') Sister plant to 'Applecross' and almost identical, raised from seed given to Dennis by Jack Ballard. The well-shaded pips are bright-crimson contrasting well with the gold centre. An excellent grower that offsets freely but appears to have fallen out of favour.

Shergold (A. Hawkes, 1979, 'Tintoretto' x 'Blossom') A golden-brown variety from that prolific raiser Allan Hawkes.

Sirius (F. Jacques, 1979) The most controversial variety at the present time due to its abrupt colour shading, from purple-maroon to pale-primrose. The bright gold centre is often marred by the body colour encroaching on it. Like most colour breaks, 'Sirius' is flawed in some respects but has provided a launching pad for raisers from which to produce many new prize-winning seedlings.

Sir John (A. Hawkes, 1986, 'Sirius' x 'Prince John') A vigorous new seedling, maroon markedly shaded to a buff edge but with a well-defined bright gold centre. The form is superior to its seed parent 'Sirius'. A possible fault is the tendency to over-offset, although it still produces a showable truss.

Snooty Fox (D. Telford, 1978) Named after a hostelry in Solihull close to the Show Hall. A large truss of dark-red pips shaded to burnt orange is possible. At times the petals are not quite flat and the centre uneven. This plant was thought to have died out, but stock was then rediscovered.

Snooty Fox 2nd (D. Telford, 1982) Derek named this plant 'Snooty Fox 2nd' after he believed the original was extinct. The first then reappeared! Similar in colouring; dark red shading to golden-orange.

Tarantella (D. Telford, 1979) Another orange-red seedling that grows well and is freely available.

Ted Roberts (J. Allen, 1977) A plant with dark-red flowers, shading almost imperceptibly. The pips tend to fade as they age, giving a two-tone appearance.

Valerie Clare (D. Telford, 1987) A lovely deep golden-brown seedling that won the Riddle seedling trophy at the Northern show.

Verdi (H. Lennie, 1943) One of the older varieties now lacking in vigour and probably affected by virus. A famous variety in its day that won several Premiers. A lovely golden colour but noted for having traces of paste in the centre.

Winnifrid (F. Faulkner, 1950, 'Tom Jones' x 'Irene') One of Frank Faulkner's finest seedlings, a leading variety for many years. In colour a beautiful crimson shading to bright scarlet. A good grower but less prominent on the show bench in recent years, though still voted sixth in the 1992 Midland and West Top Sixes.

List of Light-Centre Varieties

Adrian (A. Delbridge, 1970) A robust grower with neat pointed leaves that is freely available. The medium-sized pips are dark violet, shading dramatically to light lilac.

Alicia (F. Bailey, 1979, 'Frank Crosland' x 'Joy') A lovely, bright medium-purple shaded pink with a small cream centre. A robust grower that is freely available.

Ann Taylor (R. Taylor, 1979, Douglas seed) A good blue, shading to almost white, similar in colouring to Frank Crosland.

Argus (J. Keen, 1887) The oldest variety, still vigorous and winning prizes. A unique colour of dark plum shading to beetroot with a centre that can be less than clear-cut on occasion. The colour and form can vary according to growing conditions but still, after over 100 years, it is capable of being grown to Premier standard. 'Argus' has been micropropagated and so is freely available. However, the resulting plants show a distressing tendency to over-offset, as do most tissue-cultured plants. Voted best light centre in the Midland and West Top Sixes in both 1990 and 1991.

Avril Hunter (D. Telford, 1988) Another seedling cup winner, almost-blue colouring shading to near-white. A promising variety with fine large pips.

C. W. Needham (P. Johnson, 1934) Sumptuous, dark purple-blue pips, only moderately shaded with a small centre and a neatly fretted tube. The centre can be angular on occasion but this fault is intermittent. Still a vigorous grower with attractive serrated foliage, it offsets adequately. Like 'Argus', this plant has been micropropagated with the same resulting forest of offsets. Percy Johnson was gardener to Mr Shipman and then Mr Thompson, both prominent members of the Northern Section at that time. C. W. Needham was a member of the Northern Section for many years, serving as a judge from 1925, and was a cousin of the famous Sam Barlow.

Divint Dunch (D. Telford, 1990) Derek hails from the North East and the name is a Geordie phrase meaning 'don't push'. The pips are medium-sized and the colouring is similar to 'Sandra'.

Doris Jean (F. Jacques, 1975, 'Rowena' x 'Peggy') The flower has three distinct zones of colour: dark red, rose and pink. A desirable plant but difficult to obtain and an unreliable grower. Awarded Premier on its first appearance and again in 1984. Frank named it after his wife, who was treasurer of the Northern Section for a time.

Elsie May (D. Telford, 1972) The flowers shade from deep plum, and the velvety colour fades as the pips age; this makes it difficult to get a precise truss. The small pale centre can also be imprecise. The colour is very similar to 'Joy', a famous old variety. Featured in both the 1990 and 1991 Midland and West Top Sixes.

Frank Crosland (C. F. Faulkner, 1930) A striking variety that produces a small number of large sumptuous pips, dark blue-purple with a sharply contrasting ice-blue edge. Although old and less vigorous, this is the variety by which the newer near-blues are measured.

Enlightened (D. Telford, 1990) A new seedling from Derek which he thinks highly of.

Gordon Douglas (J. Douglas, 1918, 'Roxborough' x 'Mrs Berkeley') Some twenty years ago this was the leading light centre, a legendary plant that won numerous Premier awards. The colour is deep violet-blue shaded lighter, with a cream centre that is sometimes angular. When Buckley's collection was purchased by Dr Duthie it included a fine stock of 'Gordon Douglas', of a vigour superior to the other clones then in circulation. Vigour has now declined and it is a shadow of its former self.

Jeannie Telford (D. Telford, 1977) A lovely variety with large pips that Derek named after his wife. The flowers are a cerise colour with correct shading. The centre is on the large side with a nicely fretted tube.

John Wayne (L. Bailey, 1979, 'Frank Crosland' x 'Joy') A superb plant capable of Premier-type trusses. The large pips of medium plum shade to a lighter edge and the small, neat cream centre has a fretted tube. After initial introduction, when it was much acclaimed, it was nearly lost to cultivation and acquired a reputation for being difficult. However 'John Wayne' has now become established and has featured in the Midland and West Top Sixes for the last five years.

Joy (P. Johnson, 1931) Percy Johnson raised this plant when he was gardener to Mr Thompson at Altringham in Cheshire. A famous plant described by Dr Newton as 'an auricula of substance' with many Premiers to its credit. The pips are a deep reddish crimson with a rich velvety texture. They are inclined to cockle, as the petals ridge up, and the shading is often deficient. Still a good easy grower and has proved a successful parent.

Kevin Keegan (D. Telford, 1983) Crimson shading to pink with a very white centre.

Lady Daresbury (C. F. Faulkner, 1931) A large plant with a tall stem that produces large pips of a wine-red colour, beautifully shaded to cerise and a cream centre. Another famous plant which Dr Newton described in the 1960s as 'the most handsome and attractive Alpine auricula'. From the same cross as 'Peggy', at that time it was frequently first in the single class and was awarded several Premiers. Vigour had deteriorated, with plants reduced to a single spike during winter until, some years ago, Eddie Picken had it micropropagated. The resulting plants now grow normally. This plant was named after Lady Daresbury, at the time Patron of the Northern Society.

Lisa (D. Telford, 1978) A vigorous variety that grows into a large plant. The medium to large flat pips have a narrow, deep purple body colour shading to a wide edge of pale lilac.

Margaret Faulkner (F. Faulkner, 1953, 'Joy' x 'Gordon Douglas') A classical variety that is now less vigorous than formerly. Premier-type trusses with well-formed pips of dark-plum red and distinctive pale foliage. One of Frank Faulkner's finest seedlings.

Mark (D. Telford, 1972, 'Thetis' x 'Rowena') A large plant producing fine trusses of many decently-sized pips. Its bright pink colour and classical shading make it the leading light centre in recent years, although surprisingly both 'Argus' and 'Sandra' have achieved higher positions in recent Midland and West Top Sixes. It tends to have a large white centre that can be spoiled if the petal edges cut in. This variety has been grown in the garden where it forms a large clump. A very fine exhibition variety of Premier quality.

Mrs L. Hearn (J. Douglas, 1939) A small plant that has lost vigour, almost certainly due to age. The small trusses produce small pips with a unique colour of violet-blue shading to a wide edge of pale 'auricula' blue.

Although not regarded as a show plant any longer, it shares with 'Walton' the distinction of being the nearest true blue auricula.

Paragon (H. Burbridge, 1952) A small plant that can produce a neat truss of plum-purple pips shading lighter. On occasion the centre can be faulty but this is not always the case. When on form, this is a good plant for the show bench.

Phyllis Douglas (J. Douglas, 1909) A very old variety, thought extinct for years, that miraculously reappeared. Since then it has enjoyed a new lease of life and has become widely distributed. An early bloomer, it regularly produces a good truss of dark purple pips shading lighter. The petals are nicely rounded and a small neat centre completes the picture.

Rabley Heath (A. Hawkes, 1972) A small but vigorous plant that has dark-blue pips with a narrow light-blue edge, giving almost a picotee effect.

Rowena (J. Stant, 1967) A small plant that is different: it has medium-sized pips of purple-violet shading to a wide edge of pale lilac. The colouring is very delicate and this, together with a refined cream centre, makes it most attractive and desirable. A reasonably good grower, it produces a good supply of offsets.

Roxborough (J. Douglas, 1902) A superb old variety with large flat pips of dark, deep purple, suffusing to a narrow edge of light violet with a small neat centre. When well grown, this plant can still produce a large truss.

Sandra (H. A. Cohen, 1973) A Southern grower, Mr H. Warriner, sent seed to Hal Cohen who raised this lovely seedling. It can be grown to Premier standard with a refined truss of exquisite eight-petalled pips that are normally slightly cupped. The colour is a fine mauve shading lighter with a small, well-defined centre. When exhibited it must be shown fresh, because the colour changes as the pips age. Voted first in the 1992 Midland and West Top Sixes, it has at least three Premier awards.

Valerie (A. Hawkes, 1967, Unnamed seedling x 'Paragon') A vigorous, free-flowering plant, beautifully shading from dark to light mauve.

Vee-Too (A. Hawkes, 1967, Unnamed seedling x 'Paragon') From the same seed pod as 'Valerie' and very similar in colouring.

Victoria De Wemyss (D. Telford, 1982) Raised by J. Wemyss-Cooke from a tray of unflowered seedlings given him by Derek Telford. A large, vigorous plant with good trusses of dark blue-purple shading almost white. The colour is that near-blue shade unique to the auricula. Voted third in the 1992 Midland and West Top Sixes.

Vulcan (F. Faulkner, 1955, 'Joy' x 'Peggy') A robust plant with dark green foliage. The flat pips are a dark, reddish purple-blue with a narrow lilac edge. The centre is small but can sometimes be faulty with the tube on the large side. Frank Faulkner named it for his father, who was a smith.

Walton (G. Douglas, pre-1960) An old plant also known as 'Lady Lavender'. Arguably still the nearest to true blue (with the possible exception of 'Mrs L. Hearn'). A favourite of its raiser, but unsuitable for exhibition due to an imperfect centre.

4 Double Auriculas

Double auriculas, as their name suggests, have more petals than the normal five, six, seven or exceptionally eight of the single-flowered auricula. The amount of doubling varies, with some flowers only slightly double, some with one extra row of petals, and others that are an amorphous mass. However, they all have extra petals obscuring the centre tube. Unless these centre petals are present the flowers are considered semi-double, inferior and unacceptable; the gap in the centre is unpleasant to look at.

Double auriculas were amongst the first novelties grown by early Florists and are mentioned in gardening books of the seventeenth century. The earliest written reference to a double is by John Rea in his *Flora* (published 1665), although paintings by Alexander Marshall, a noted floral artist, show that doubles, including some that were striped, were being grown earlier. Some of the most prized doubles changed hands for high prices. One is recorded as costing £20, a very high price for such a small plant – even today. When the show auriculas came into prominence in about 1750, the double and striped auriculas fell out of fashion, becoming very rare.

John MacWatt, in his classic work *The Primulas of Europe*, published in 1923, mentions several different doubles including the 'rare old Double Yellow', 'Double Green', 'Double Blue', and even a 'charming Double Grey'. He then went on to say that 'To the strait-laced florist devoted to the stage Auricula these double flowers are monstrosities but they are interesting flowers all the same'.

In Ireland the legendary Miss W. F. Wynne raised a number of new doubles, while growing some of the rare survivors from an earlier era such as the 'Double Green'. She raised, among others, 'Avoca Apricot', 'Tawny', 'Red-Brown' and 'Crimson'. Later she grew a seedling from the 'Double Green' named 'Glaslanna' or 'Green Child'. Miss Wynne was famous both in England and in America; seed and pollen from her plants was sent or taken to both countries. Miss Wynne also grew what she described as 'the very rare old striped red and white Auricula, 'Mrs Dargan', thought to be the last survivor of a once greatly admired section of striped auriculas'. She then went on to say 'When properly grown the blossom is double … Regrettably, it often blossoms single or with only one or two double flowers in the truss'. This plant, or one claiming to be it, has survived to the present day in a degenerated form. The flowers are very small and ragged, with only an occasional extra petal to suggest it may once have been a double, although traces of striping are evident.

In 1948 Sir Roland Biffen wrote in his book *The Auricula* that 'Double auriculas form a group which is almost lost to cultivation ... so rare are they that most Auricula growers had never seen a specimen.' Roy Genders' book

Auriculas (1958) dismisses them in one paragraph, mentioning that he had seen only two. At this time the modern resurgence of the doubles was beginning in America. By 1958 plants and seed had come over to Britain and a new wave of enthusiasm was under way.

To understand how double flowers of any sort arise it is necessary to know a little about the science of genetics which has risen to prominence this century. Towards the end of the last century an Austrian monk, Gregor Mendel, discovered by experiments, mostly on peas, how inherited characteristics in living things are handed down from one generation to another.

The papers outlining his work and deductions lay forgotten for some years but their rediscovery in 1900 eventually gave rise to the branch of the biological science we call genetics.

Sir Roland Biffen, FRS, an eminent geneticist at Cambridge University who was working to improve wheat strains, was also interested in auriculas. Luckily he applied his scientific knowledge to them, and wrote a fascinating book, *The Auricula: The Story of a Florists' Flower*, published posthumously in 1951. In it he explained numerous scientific facets of auricula growing, many of which have been incorporated here. Auricula breeders were then able to understand the mechanics of doubling and began hybridizing to raise new varieties. Prior to this double auriculas arose only by chance. Offsets of chance seedlings were grown and passed on to other raisers, but most auriculas have only a finite life and in time varieties would become extinct.

The doubling of any flower comes about through an inborn genetic tendency for the sexual parts of the flower to become replaced by petals. The scientific phrase is that they become 'petaloid'. Double flowers do occur in the wild – a double buttercup on a mountainside in Switzerland has been seen but they are rare because they are unable to reproduce themselves. In cultivation double flowers are quite common. Indeed in carnations, roses, chrysanthemums and many other flowers they are more common and admired than single flowers. The majority of double-flower plants are those that have radial symmetry and the auricula is one of this company. A well-flowered auricula pip has frequently been compared to a small single rose (although the way the flower is held on its stalk is different).

It is due to enthusiasts in America, in particular Ralph Balcom and Mrs Denna Snuffer, that we have double auriculas today; indeed the double section is the fastest-growing group of all auriculas. Ralph Balcom's keen eye discovered a solitary purple double, one bloom, growing quite by chance amongst a large group of border auriculas he had raised from seed. Realising its potential he used pollen from it on four other single plants, a yellow, red and two different purples.

Balcom related, in an article he wrote for the Southern Section year book, that the first generation of seedlings were all single. The gene for doubling is recessive, as opposed to that for the single (explained later), and it was only in the second generation seedlings that the desired double flowers reappeard. He then met a fellow American also working on doubles, Mrs Denna Snuffer, and they exchanged plants. Mrs Snuffer had become interested in auriculas following the Second World War, during which she lost both her sons, and obtained seed from England of any type of auricula she could find. Her first double blossom also arose spontaneously and this set her on her mission which, at a later stage, involved growing over 1,000 doubles! Their colours were generally pale, lacking brightness and tending to fade on opening. Ralph Balcom's strain contained brighter colours

Single
Dominant gene 'S'

Double
Recessive gene 'd'

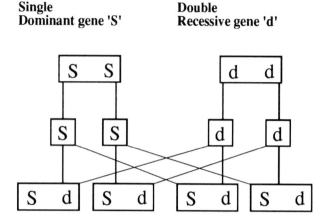

Parent generation
28 chromosomes [28]
14 from one parent
14 from the other
Sex cells, the paired
genes separate   [14]
F1 generation, each
one inherits a gene
from each parent [28]
All carry the doubling
gene but appear single

Any 2 parents of the F1 generation may be chosen by the hybridiser

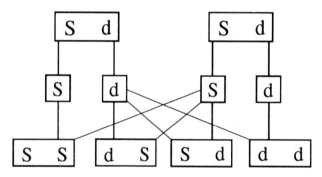

F1 parents   [28]
Sex cells   [14]
The genes separate
Any cell may be
fertilised by any other
from other parent
F2 generation [28]

On average:
One seedling is SS - a pure single
Two seedlings are Sd - look single but carry the recessive gene for doubling
One seedling is dd - The doubling reappears in the 2nd generation
For one gene the odds are 1 out of 4
For two genes the odds are 1 out of 16 (4 x 4)

GENETICS OF DOUBLING

which he crossed with the Snuffer strain, naming the resulting plants 'Denna Doubles'. Articles appeared in the American Primrose Society quarterly journal and plants were brought back to England by Dr Lester-Smith, given to him by Mrs Snuffer when he was on a business trip to America in 1958. He shared some with Kenneth Gould, at that time Treasurer of the Southern Section, who was also in contact with Ralph Balcom, and it was these two growers who were mainly responsible for the revival of doubles in England. From this seed the double auriculas 'Mary' and 'Catherine' were raised in 1961. Both these plants were primrose yellow in colour and are still in cultivation today; other varieties were also raised at this time. These two varieties, from the same seed capsule, are involved in the parentage of many strains available today.

Double-flowered plants of other types discovered growing wild have been collected, cultivated in gardens and propagated by division. That is undoubtedly how the double primroses mentioned in old herbals came into being. Now we have the ability to produce double auriculas from seed and while only a some seedlings will be double, up to twenty-five per cent, a small number will be sufficiently attractive to propagate and distribute.

The mechanics of pollination are explained in detail in Chapter 7. The principles of hand pollination are that the parents should be chosen to achieve the desired attributes in the resultant seedlings. For example, a plant with a good colour might be crossed with one that has fine form, in the hope that a seedling with improved form and colour will result.

In auriculas the stamens and/or the pistil may be replaced by extra petals. This naturally precludes the plant from producing seed. The genes for doubling of stamens and pistil are recessive. In any organism, plant or animal, the genes that determine an individual's characteristics are inherited in pairs, one from each parent. One gene usually has a stronger influence on the appearance of the offspring than the other; this gene is said to be dominant. The weaker gene is called recessive. Recessive means that the characteristic of this gene is hidden or disappears, overridden by the effect of its stronger partner. However, recessive genes are still present in the gametes, sex cells that carry a parent's genetic material in the form of chromosomes (strings of genes). A parent's genes settle in a random fashion on the chromosomes. Each gene appears only once in each gamete. When two parents' gametes join during reproduction, they combine to form a new individual: chromosomes join in pairs to recombine genes in a new and unique way. If two recessive genes, one from each parent, carrying the same characteristic meet, that characteristic will appear in the offspring. Many congenital human diseases, such as haemophilia, are caused by recessive genes.

In humans, it is well known that a child may inherit his or her maternal grandmother's eye colour and paternal grandfather's physique. In auriculas, if genes for both double and single flowers are present, the flower will be single, as this gene is dominant. The first generation of such a cross is called the first filial generation, or F1 for short. If two of the offspring, F1 hybrids, are then crossed together to form a second (F2) generation, both parent plants carry the hidden doubling gene as well as the single gene. On average one seedling will carry two single genes: two will carry one single and one double gene but will appear single. Finally, in the fourth seedling both genes will be double and this plant will produce double flowers. That is the theory. This is only a statistical probability and large numbers of plants have to be grown to demonstrate it, beyond the capacity of most amateurs. In the small numbers of seedlings that it is practical for most raisers to grow, the figures may be distorted, more often in favour of dominant-gene characteristic.

If one parent of a seedling is double, it is practically certain that all the offspring will carry the gene for doubling although the flowers may appear single. Such a plant is called a heterozygote, meaning that it carries genes for alternative (hetero- = different) characteristics. If two siblings known from their parentage to be heterozygous are crossed, it is likely that a full double will result in the next generation. It has recently been discovered that the Alpine auricula 'Sirius' is such a heterozygote. Cliff Timpson of Lichfield informs us that his red double seedling 'Corrie Files' is a 'Sirius' seedling, something no one would imagine simply from looking at the parent plant.

Many more factors than double petals make a first-class double auricula: attractive colour, smooth outline to petals, strong footstalks, good constitution, ability to offset reasonably; but there is, of course, no guarantee that all these will be combined with doubling. Nor, unfortunately, is there any guarantee that the doubling will be complete, as there is evidence that more than one gene is involved. The doubling genes may be separated at the gamete stage, producing flowers that have open centres or are semi-double – undesirable except for further hybridizing.

At least two separate, recessive genes are involved in the doubling process, that for double anthers and that for the stigma. As the degree of doubling of both sex organs can vary from one seedling to another, it is likely that more than two pairs of genes are involved. The hybridizing of doubles has been carried out mainly by amateur growers, Thousands of plants would have to be raised in order to provide truly reliable statistics on these different points.

If it is looked for carefully, some pollen can usually be found even where the stamens (male organs) have been almost entirely replaced by extra petals. Some very full doubles, where the female sex organs have become petaloid, have deformed stigmas and are unable to bear seed. However, some of the varieties with fewer petals do have perfect stigmas deep down in the floral tube that can and do produce fertile seed. If such a plant is hand pollinated with pollen from a flower with petaloid anthers there are sure to be some double seedlings. 'Mary', raised in 1961 by Ken Gould, is an example of a double flower with a functional stigma, and has been used by at least two different hybridizers.

Some named varieties of single auriculas frequently produce a single petaloid anther (the pollen-bearing tip of the stamen). This is usually a sign that those particular plants have some tendency to doubling. Several plants, notably the Alpine 'Gordon Douglas' and the selfs 'Oakes Blue' and 'Remus', have been used as pollinators in the quest for doubles. There is also evidence that plants with ruffled petals may carry double genes. Such flowers are not accepted except in border classes, but one border auricula, 'Old Irish Blue', which owes much of its beauty to very full, fluted petals, has thrown double and semi-double seedlings.

When a new double variety flowers for the first time, it is useful to pull a spent flower apart to discover if a perfect stigma is present and if it too can be used to develop new varieties. Sometimes the stigma is not like a pin with one head, but branched. Several rudimentary 'pins' take its place and it is inadvisable to use such plants as seed parents. In extreme cases the ovary wall is incomplete, so any seeds that are fertilized and begin developing dry out before they are mature and do not develop full term. Sometimes developing petaloid stigmas can be seen bursting out of the tube like a small stubby paint brush, developing into petals as they grow: this occurrence has been photographed. Such flowers are unable to set seed but they may possibly bear pollen and could be used as a pollen parent. As the particular plant photographed had single anthers it was not a pretty sight, but has proved a valuable parent.

In September 1992, Dr Martin Sheader of Southampton, currently President of the Southern Section, gave a lecture on double auriculas. He showed a remarkable series of photographs taken through a microscope, showing many different flowers in various stages of conversion, of both male and female parts, into petals. Many of the points described above were illustrated in these slides.

Double auriculas are still at an early stage of their reintroduction. Thirty years' random development is a short time in such a quest. Many hybridizers tend to be satisfied with a flower showing full doubling, without regard for its colouring, or for the outline of the petals. Others regard impure, muddy colours and notched petals as faults, keeping only those seedlings with a pleasing pure colour and smooth outline to the petals. Naturally, this insistence on good form further reduces the number of acceptable seedlings.

It has also been discovered that the old maxim 'breed like with like' applies to colour. The result of ten years' line breeding by Gwen Baker, seeking a red double, is a dark-red seedling, 'Doyen', not the bright scarlet sought but a true red with no hint of purple. Unfortunately pure red colouring also seems to be recessive. A pip of 'Doyen' in its first flowering was pulled to pieces but neither pollen nor stigma were found; all were converted to petals, and it looked like the end of the line. In its second year an immature offset bore flowers that were not fully double and a search discovered pollen that may enable this line to continue.

Breeding new varieties is fraught with frustration and disappointment, but the excitement and euphoria when a good new variety flowers makes everything worthwhile. The sense of expectation when seedlings are starting to flower is enormous and auricula growers are born optimists.

Over the last thirty years more growers have taken up the challenge of trying to raise double auriculas and today there is a better range of colours available, though there is still room for improvement. Most of the first wave of doubles were cream, yellow and brown and these colours still dominate, with many new varieties in these shades, although there are now some good purples becoming more widely available. In red, colours are still on the dark side; one raised by Len Bailey, called 'Matthew Yates', is so dark that it appears black. There are also others of a reddish purple, an attractive pink ('Pink Fondant', raised by Tim Coop), while 'Susannah' from Allan Hawkes is a cool lilac pink. A striped double, aptly named 'Stripey', has been raised by Derek Salt and a seedling from it a cream and pink picotee. A line of breeding still explored by more than one hybridizer is the quest for a good scarlet double. With many of these new varieties, there are still few plants in circulation but it is hoped, in time, that they will become more readily available.

Colour apart, there are at least two types of double auricula with different form. One has the symmetrical doubling commonly seen in camellias, with a large number of petals laid one over another very regularly and most satisfying to the eye, for example 'Thirlmere' and 'Gwen Baker'. These are known as 'classical' doubles. The other class, 'non-classical'

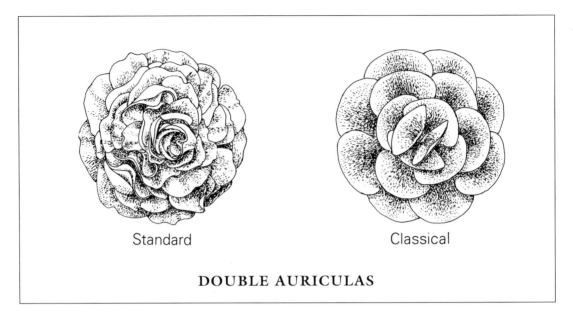

Standard   Classical

DOUBLE AURICULAS

doubles, have a much coarser lay of petals, some crinkled, for instance 'Golden Char-treuse', a Barnhaven seedling (see p. 65), and 'Marigold', rather like a French marigold, which has a unique colour between gold and brown. It is possible that the doubles from Allan Hawkes and the seedlings from these, 'Susannah', 'Doublure' and 'Walton Heath', show another type of doubling. Very full and regular, imbricate, quartered like a Gallicia rose, they are usually regarded as classical in form, but should more be raised, they may eventually form a third type.

There remains some controversy over what other characteristics an acceptable double auricula should have, for example whether plants shaded like Alpine auriculas are attrac-tive or even desirable. There is also disagree-ment over the degree of doubling and the number of extra petals a flower should have before it is classed as a double. One school believes in a minimum of two rows of petals, another that the number of extra petals is immaterial so long as the centre is decently covered. Both sides agree, however, that the

central boss of petals should completely hide the floral tube that is so prominent in other auriculas, and that an 'open-centred' plant should be regarded only as semi-double.

One point of excellence on which agree-ment has been reached is that the degree of doubling should be the same for all the flow-ers in a truss. If the extent of doubling varies from pip to pip, this is a fault. In some plants the first few blossoms are double, the next to open are semi-double and the last are com-pletely or almost single. This is often a sign that the plant has had too lean a diet; it also means that the end flowers are more likely to have functional stigmas and stamens and still carry the gene or genes for doubling. These flowers can be used as seed parents for devel-oping new varieties.

Another fault often found in doubles is that a very full pip is too heavy. Certain varieties tend to hang their heads because the foot-stalks are not strong enough or too drawn to hold the blossoms upright. This is generally caused by incorrect growing conditions – probably lack of light causing the footstalks to grow long and thin, poor compost, or both. 'Doublet', raised by Allan Hawkes, sometimes shows this characteristic yet is hardy and sturdy enough to be grown as a border. In the garden the footstalks are always short and strong and the plant holds its head high. That it can be grown to this standard in a greenhouse has been proved by the examples seen occasionally on the show bench.

There is no doubt that double auriculas respond to additional feeding, enabling them to fashion their extra petals. They respond well to a dose of nitrogenous fertilizer administered when growth starts in mid-February, about a week after they are given their first watering. Apart from this, double auriculas require similar cultivation to Alpine auriculas. Both can be grown in the same greenhouse using the same methods.

One of the most delightful attributes of double auriculas is their delicate perfume, in many ways similar to a cowslip or wild primrose. Most of the other, more inbred types have lost this characteristic, in the same way that many roses have. Border auriculas have scent in abundance and luckily so do many doubles. This scent is most noticeable early in the morning; it is a pleasure to enter the greenhouse while the dew is still wet on the grass, the perfume heavy in the air. Many people have mentioned this as one of the benefits of growing doubles.

Because the number of good double auriculas is still restricted, this is a very attractive field for hybridizing. There is a number of growers currently engaged in it. Prominent hybridizers include Dr Martin Sheader, Derek Salt, Len Bailey, Keith Leeming, Ken Whorton, Martin and Dreena Thompson and Gwen Baker. They normally hand-pollinate (see Chapter 7), choosing the parents carefully.

This chapter would not be complete without mentioning that the firm of Barnhaven have been producing double auricula seed for many years. Barnhaven was first established in Oregon, USA by Florence Bellis, continued by Jared Sinclair and his wife in Cumbria and most recently by Angela Bradford, who has moved the Barnhaven operation to France. This firm is noted mainly for polyanthus seed, of which the most famous is the Cowichan strain, and also for double primroses. They also produce seed of many other primulas, including double auriculas. As this is a commercial undertaking, the seed is hand pollinated but the choice of parents is arbitrary and the resulting seedlings are not intended for exhibition but for garden decoration. The Barnhaven doubles show many characteristics, like notched petals and impure colours, which make most of them unsuitable for the show bench. In spite of this, some attractive flowers have been raised and at least two are listed below.

STANDARDS OF PERFECTION

Meritorious
- *Foliage* that is well-balanced, crisp and healthy.
- *Flower Stem* that is strong; sufficiently long to bear the truss well above the foliage.
- *Truss* that is carried on pedicels long enough to avoid overcrowding and sufficiently strong to prevent the pips from drooping.
- *Pips* that are of rich or clear colours.
- *Doubling* that is symmetrical and fills the corolla effectively.
- *All pips* to possess the same degree of doubling.
- *Petals* with a round, smooth outline, without notches and serrations.

Defective

- *Foliage* that is limp, unbalanced or unhealthy.
- *A stem* that is weak or short.
- *Pedicels* that allow the pip to be overcrowded or to droop.
- *Pips* that are not rich or clear coloured; which are muddy in colour.
- *Doubling* that is asymmetric, lacking effect, or possessing a defect whereby the doubling shows a marked decrease from the earliest to the latest pip, or where the centre is not covered.
- *Petal edges* that are notched or serrated.

A LIST OF SOME DESIRABLE DOUBLES

There are two types of double auriculas: old and new, vigorous well-distributed plants, which are easy to obtain; a second group that do not seem to be in general distribution, perhaps because they are difficult, or are new seedlings that will join the first type when stocks have accumulated. As the majority of auricula hybridizers are amateurs, new seedlings circulate slowly from hand to hand and are listed separately, for the benefit of enthusiasts.

List of Varieties

Albury (W. Hecker, 1972) A darkish red-purple, vigorous, good form, slow to develop to flowering size. Similar to 'Shalford'.
Camelot (A. Hawkes, 1967, 'Nigel' x 'South Barrow') A vigorous dark red, becoming purple with age. The footstalks tend to be rather weak and cannot hold the very full pips upright, unless well fed and grown in good light. Produces many offsets which root well; freely available, grows well in the garden.
Catherine (K. Gould, 1961, Balcom seed) An old variety with good form, lemon-yellow,

brighter than its sister 'Mary'. It has long thin leaves and the footstalks need good light to prevent them becoming drawn. Produces plenty of offsets which root well, but an old plant tends to rot easily.
Delilah (G. Baker, 1979) A deep, dark red, with no purple in its colouring. As it ages farina appears on the top of the petals which spoils the initial beauty. Vigorous and easy.
Devon Cream (unknown) Just like its name-sake, a creamy double with a golden centre, widely available through tissue culture. Rather rough form compared to the better pale yellows; possibly from Barnhaven seed.
Diamond (G. Baker, 1977) Pale cream, almost white, with a pale-green centre. Petals are broad and well shaped, only one row of petals plus a centre boss. Offsets readily and grows well, tends to come semi-double or even single if not grown well. A good seed parent, setting seed readily. Already awarded at least four Premiers.
Doublet (A. Hawkes, *c.* 1975) A very full dark-red double, offsetting freely. Vigorous enough to succeed outside in the garden and needs good light for its footstalks to support the pips.
Doublure (A. Hawkes, *c.* 1980 'Susannah' x 'Walton Heath') Similar colour to 'Doublet', a very dark red, but holds its truss more upright, like a Gallicia rose. Received a Premier on its first showing. Offsets slowly and has a tendency to rot off.
Doyen (G. Baker, 1982) Dark red, brighter than 'Delilah' and the result of ten years' line breeding. Doubling good but almost totally sterile. Vigorous, offsets well.
Eureka (G. Baker, 1982) The first pure-purple seedling. Offsets well, needs feeding but has good form, functional stigma. Tends to have only five petals in a row.
Fandango (G. Baker, 1983) Excellent double form, with well-rounded petals, classical

form and extraordinary colour, altering with temperature. Varying from rose-purple to pure deep purple depending on growing conditions.

Frank Bailey (L. Bailey, *c.* 1970) A large-flowered, very full, brownish-golden double that grows vigorously.

Gaia (M. Sheader, 1974, 'Barnhaven seed') A full double the colour of old ivory, creamy buff. Vigorous, offsets well.

Golden Chartreuse (G. Black, *c.* 1970, 'Barnhaven seed') Another Barnhaven seedling, a lovely golden colour, rather rough form but nevertheless a winner. A strong healthy grower.

Golden Splendour (L. Bailey, 1987, 'Frank Bailey' seedling) A recent winning seedling still in short supply. Burnished gold, more brown than 'Frank Bailey'. Vigorous, offsets freely, has excellent form.

Guinea Gold (H. A. Cohen, 1979, 'Barnhaven seed') A vigorous variety, bright gold as its name suggests. This was the best gold shade for some years.

Gwen Baker (D. Salt, 1988) Shown as a seedling at an RHS show where it created so much interest that it was named. A large vigorous plant, pale yellow, that is slow to offset. In order to increase stock the top can be cut off. Premier in 1993 at both Knowle and Brompton. As it has been tissue cultured it should be available.

Helena Dean (L. Bailey, 1979) Very similar in shape and colouring to 'Jane Myers'.

Jane Myers I and II (L. Bailey, 1976, 'Barnhaven seed' x 'Mary') Two very similar, lovely varieties, full classical doubling on a large truss. Difficult to obtain and grow, as both rot easily, but worth every effort; they make excellent parents for new varieties. Number one seemed to have died off but resurrected itself after number two was named.

Lima (K. Whorton, 1989, 'Hoghton Gem' x 'Mary') Lime yellow, a large truss with comparatively small pips, offsets freely. A stocky medium-sized plant. Premier at Saltford in 1993.

Maid Marion (K. Gould, 1964) A well-formed full double, pale-primrose in colour. It offsets freely but is liable to rot.

Marigold (R. Newton, *c.* 1960, F2 seedling 'Meeks Double' x 'Minstead') An extraordinary flower, very full and crinkled petals the colour of mustard. The pollen parent was a Haysom green edge and that lover of green edges, Fred Buckley, gave it its name. A very full double with no real shape to the flower; arouses strong feelings, both for and against. This was a plant that rarely produced an offset but tissue culture has made it readily available.

Mary (K. Gould, 1961, 'Balcom seed') Pale primrose yellow, one of the oldest of the 'new' doubles still grown but remaining vigorous. Easy to grow and offsets well. 'Mary' has been used extensively in breeding new varieties, setting seed readily.

Matthew Yates (L. Bailey, *c.* 1980) A very dark, almost black, red with a full corolla, making a good tight truss. A vigorous grower that offsets freely. A good exhibition variety.

Megan (L. Bailey, 1982) A late-flowering variety, of a burnt sienna colour with full pips on a strong stem. A vigorous growing variety that tends to have a leafy calyx, not opening properly.

Mipsie Miranda (H. Wood, 1982, 'Jane Myers' seedling) Similar to its parent with the same full doubling.

Moonstone (G. Baker, 1980) A lemon-yellow, with good doubling and shape, making a neat truss. Offsets well and grows easily.

Pink Fondant (G. Coop, 1979) The best pink double, at its best a beautiful variety. Offsets reasonably well but still scarce as the old plant rots easily. The petals are sometimes serrated and the pip can be open centred.

Sarah Lodge (R. Cole, 1980) The true plant has rose-purple, well-formed pips with rounded petals. There is, however, an imposter in circulation with the same name that is more vigorous and a darker purple.

Shalford (W. Hecker, *c.* 1970) An early double, very similar in colouring (dark purple-red) and form to 'Albury'.

Sir Robert (Lester-Smith, *c.* 1960) Also known as 'Sir Robert Ewbank'. The first pink double to be raised that is always open centred. At least one Premier award in 1968.

South Barrow (K. Gould, 1962) Another early plant, very similar in colour to 'Doublet' that tends to hang its head.

Standish (A. Guest, *c.* 1970) Pale-buff double with serrated petals, doubling only fair.

Stripey (D. Salt, 1985) An attempt to recreate the old striped doubles from an earlier century. The pips tend to be smaller than those of other doubles but it carries a good number of primrose-yellow pips streaked and striped with purple. Offsets readily, a curiosity.

Susannah (A. Hawkes, *c.* 1960) A pale lilac-pink, excellent doubling like a quartered old-fashioned rose. Offsets freely and a vigorous grower. In photographs a most desirable pink, but in reality has more blue in its make-up, near to French lilac. Offsets must be controlled to get a decent truss.

The Cardinal (unknown) This is the plant reputed to have come from the garden of Cardinal Richlieu in France. It is a dull crimson and a fair double.

Thirlmere (G. Baker, 1984) Rather a dull purple, excellent form, offsets well. First shown as a border double with multiple trusses as it had been growing in the garden. Premier Brompton 1992.

Trouble (D. Salt, 1988) One of two seedlings; the other, 'Strife', died. It has

superb form but the controversial colour is a mixture of yellow, pink and green. It has been tissue-cultured, so is available, and has also been sold as 'Micro'.

Walton Heath (A. Hawkes, *c.* 1970) A vigorous dark-purple double with a sound constitution. It has been used successfully as a parent, passing on its purple colouring and full doubling.

Watt's Purple (unknown) An old variety, origin unknown, in existence in 1965 when it was mentioned in an article as a good pollen parent. Vigorous, offsets well.

Westcott Pride (K. Gould, 1967) A fully-double dark red, shaded flower, of Alpine descent with mealy foliage. 'Basuto' was one of the original parents. It has been used in breeding new colours.

Zambia (K. Gould, pre-1965) A dark, almost black, double, split into vigorous and weak clones, probably affected by virus.

Supplementary list

Ashwood Gold (P. Baulk, *c.* 1970) Aptly named, fully-double pips of a rich gold colour, very suitable for showing, reluctant to offset, of limited availability. Raised by P. Baulk of Ashwood Nurseries from Barnhaven seed.

Ashwood Rose (P. Baulk, *c.* 1970) Also from Ashwood and very rare, seemingly grown by only one person. Fairly typical of the Barnhaven doubles with notched petals, very full pips.

Autumnal (D. and M. Thompson, 1991) A new seedling that won a Premier on its first showing at Knowle, 1992.

Avoca Tawny (W. F. Wynne, pre-1957) Shown at Saltford, 1989, this is one of the very rare earlier doubles, raised in Eire, by the legendary Miss Wynne.

Beltane Fire (M. Sheader, 1990) Really fiery, red streaked with orange. A beautiful new seedling.

Calypso (K. Whorton, 1990) A soft orange-marmalade seedling from 'Westcott Pride'.

Cariad Bach (P. Bowen, 1986) Welsh for 'Little Darling', from Mr Bowen of Llanelli. A beautiful, glowing double pink, shaded like an Alpine. It does not appear vigorous and is still rare.

Corrie Files (C. Timpson, 1990) Another new seedling, a dark red double, almost unbelievably a seedling from the Alpine auricula 'Sirius'. Offsets well.

Digit (K. Whorton, 1992) A superb form and a lovely golden colour that won the seedling class at Knowle, 1992. Offsets readily, lanky carrot, narrow leaves.

Emberglow (M. Sheader, 1990) An orange-red, fully double with smooth-edged frilly petals. From the same seed pod as 'Beltane Fire' and 'Fireball'.

Geminae (A. Guest, 1989) A bright yellow full double that sometimes has notched petals, otherwise worth growing. It is vigorous, offsets well and throws a neat truss. Easily recognized out of flower as its leaves have pronounced rounded teeth.

Gingernut (D. and M. Thompson, 1992) Another new one from the Thompsons that was named at the Knowle show. The name describes the colour.

Gold Button (M. Sheader, 1992) Won the Premier at Saltford, 1992. A beautiful clear-yellow variety of classical form.

Kirklands (origin unknown) At least two plants are in circulation bearing this name, one not worth growing; a peculiar red-brown colour with poor form.

Kirstia Jones (L. Bailey, 1992, 'Jane Myers' x 'Walton Heath') Another seedling from that prolific raiser of doubles, Len Bailey. It has very full large pips with quartered doubling and is a light chocolate colour.

Old Double Green (unknown) A very old variety, discovered by Miss Wynne in Ireland in an old garden. A rather washy yellow-green, brownish in the centre; of poor form, of interest only for its ancient origins.

Rosamund (M. Sheader, 1991) An old-rose shade, another new seedling from Martin Sheader.

Rose Cougou (M. Sheader, 1989) A purple-mauve colour with ruffled petals. The pips are large and very full.

Sarah Brightman (D. and M. Thompson, 1991) First in the seedling class, 1991, from a 'Stripey' cross, delicately striped with red on a cream background. A really delightful plant.

Saturn (W. N. Millman, 1989) A greeny-yellow flower with few rows of petals and a centre like 'Diamond'.

Winkle (K. Gould, *c.* 1960) A rather small but exquisite pale greeny-white double.

The following have been exhibited recently. Some will become leading varieties, others may die out or deteriorate:

Northern Show: 'Charles Bronson', 'Cinnamon', 'Clifton', 'Elizabeth', 'Greswode', 'Karen', 'Malvern', 'Purple River', 'Tim Coop', 'Truffles' (or 'Ruffles').

Southern Show: 'Annuka', 'Beachcomber', 'Fishtoft', 'Naiad', 'Pompadour', 'Rosedew', 'Ruby Ball', 'Saturn'.

Midland and West Shows: 'Benington', 'Cream Blush', 'Lime'n Lemon', 'The Marquis', 'Peter Hall', 'Picottee double', 'Rose Congou', 'Sharon Hall', 'Sunscape'.

5 Border Auriculas

The least complicated type of auricula and the most widely known and grown is the 'border' or 'garden' auricula. Other old fashioned names for them are 'recklasses', 'ricklers' and 'Dusty Millers'.

There are no rules or specifications covering this group; all the odd plants that do not meet the requirements of the other types are put into this category. Some border auriculas would more properly be described as 'Miscellaneous hybrids of the Auriculastrum Section' as defined by Smith, Burrow and Lowe in *Primulas of Europe and America*. From time to time those interested in borders have attempted to set standards that define them more clearly, but so far this has met with only partial success.

If one goes for a walk around the suburbs, one often sees auriculas growing in small clumps in beds edging front lawns or paving. They are usually small unpretentious plants, blooming in spring, mainly purple or reddish flowers, occasionally yellow or buff. A sight to be remembered was once noted by one of the authors: a front garden with the small square lawn entirely surrounded with borders of bright-yellow auriculas in full flower. Border auriculas grow in Gwen Baker's east-facing front garden, and remain cool in the heat of a summer's day. They also flourish to the north of the raspberry canes, which are regularly mulched with garden compost. The goodness seems to leach out from the canes to the auriculas and they stay in flower longer than the pampered plants in the greenhouse.

Peter Ward, while heading for Scotland on a gardening holiday a few years ago in the company of two friends, saw a large number of yellow borders in the garden of a house in the small north-east fishing village of Eyemouth. The plants were growing vigorously and flowering profusely, but as no one was at home no information could be obtained (although the scene was photographed).

Borders can easily be grown from commercially available seed, in packets usually labelled 'Alpine auriculas', never 'borders'. These seeds are mainly from open-pollinated flowers cultivated in fields, and on the whole the colours tend to be rather insipid. In addition, some flowers may be misshapen and it is advisable to select the most attractive and discard the rest. New members to the National Auricula and Primula Society are advised of this and one enthusiast, Ike Hawthorn of Newbury, has grown many plants from commercial seed. His verdict was not complimentary, except for one plant he passed on to Gwen Baker. This has been seen in flower and subsequently offsets were requested by two Northern growers after it had been displayed in a border class at a show. The colour is crushed strawberry with brown bee markings around the throat. It has been named 'Bramley Rose' in honour of its raiser, who lives in Bramley Cottage.

Borders are simple unsophisticated flowers and the colours are often muted or even muddy: soft lilacs, dirty pinks, brown-reds and dull purples, sackcloth and ashes. The term is reserved for flowers that do not conform to Florists' standards. They should have strong stalks to carry the flowers well above the foliage and frequently have a trace of paste or farina in the eye of the flower. The most desirable sorts have a sweet spicy perfume, to many the 'essence of spring'.

Two main types exist which approximate in one form to show auriculas, and in the other to Alpine auriculas. In the show type the leaves are mealed and the flowers may resemble a larger or coarser show self. The other sort has meal-free leaves and flowers that are shaded. Size varies enormously; some varieties are quite small and others are much larger than the show and Alpine types. In addition, plants exist that obviously have mixed blood and fit into neither category. Some of these plants are frankly ugly, while others are more attractive and well worth growing. On occasion odd plants have appeared that were distinctive and appealing, rather than poor versions of show and Alpine auriculas.

During the centuries that this plant has been grown, particularly attractive plants have been selected, divided and passed to neighbours and occasionally to nurserymen. One such race is the 'Dusty Millers', so called for the dusting of farina or meal on their leaves. It has been noted that plants with mealy leaves are less palatable to slugs, while green-leaved varieties are eaten down to bare stumps by these pests, especially in early spring when new growth begins.

In one author's garden, a prized variety called 'Broadwell Gold' was attacked by slugs when the tender new spring growth was forming. It was not noticed in time to take preventative action and the damage was so severe the plant died (though since replaced). 'Broadwell Gold' was introduced by Joe Elliot of the famous Cotswold nursery in Broadwell village. He is supposed to have found it growing in a cottage garden in the village and obtained it from the owner. Subsequently 'Broadwell Gold' has become one of the best known of its type with vigorous golden flowers, mealy leaves and paste in the eye. Recently Richard Westwood of Cheltenham found an extremely vigorous, whitish-flowered border growing in his next-door neighbour's garden. He named it 'Mrs Harris' after the lady from whose garden it came and it has been distributed under this name. Later it was discovered that an apparently identical plant was being sold by a Scottish nursery as 'Rob Dalgleish'. This is one of the problems with borders: with many of the plants, one cannot be certain of the accuracy of their lineage. Numerous other attractive and vigorous plants have been named and indeed the National Collection holder, Mr Geoffrey Nicolle, has over 100 named varieties. It is quite common for enthusiasts to ask questions of strangers about plants they see growing in gardens; several of the named varieties owe their origins and names to such strangers' grandparents.

The cultivation of border auriculas is simple: they need well-drained, moisture-holding soil in shade or semi-shade. The long carrots that develop need to be earthed up at intervals and divided in August or September, every other year, or when they appear to need it. Like all auriculas, they are semi-dormant in winter, losing many of their leaves; they awaken in the spring to flower in April or May. As with other garden plants, new plantlets arise from the old carrots. As they elongate, these new plants fall sideways and root down where they touch the soil, like other border plants such as irises or heuchera. The old parent crown dies, leaving the new offsets to take their place, forming a clump.

As has been mentioned, slugs and snails are particular pests because some auriculas seem very attractive to them. Slug pellets in the spring give some control when the succulent young foliage is most at risk. Cover the plants with netting to prevent wild creatures or pets eating either the pellets or the dead slugs, which should be carefully disposed of. Many people do not like to use chemicals in the garden and prefer other methods, such as handpicking. One television programme recommended dropping the collected slugs into salt water. Beer traps are another option: the slugs and snails are attracted by the aroma.

Some control is necessary, otherwise serious damage may be done to the plants. For those who find bending difficult a raised bed is often useful, or one of the many planters currently available. In such an enclosed area the elimination of slugs is much easier. Derek Telford recommends Nobble, which dissolves the eggs and prevents breeding. The plants are attacked most in early spring when they, and the gardener, are emerging from their winter dormancy. At this time the small, tender new leaves can be completely eaten away.

In or about August, about three weeks before dividing the plants, it is a good idea to topdress the plants with some humus-rich soil, such as leaf mould or garden compost. Also sprinkle some bonemeal around the clumps. Then when they are ready to be divided, the new growth will have rooted into the topdressing. This makes the task easier, with the divisions ready to take hold of the new ground after a good watering. At the same time, some well-rotted manure or other humus, peat and a slow acting fertilizer can be used to enrich the bed. A sprinkling of bonemeal or hoof and horn, or one of the proprietary plant foods, such as Vitax Q4, ensure the plants have enough nourishment

for a season.

Replant when the ground is wet, after rain or when rain is expected. Never move auriculas in hot weather: the roots are reluctant to grow and the plants may fail. In the past, when horses were commonly used for transport, the practice was to mulch with well-rotted horse manure, both to feed the plants and to conserve moisture during hot, dry weather. The manure rotted down into the soil, helped by earthworms, providing well-drained soil into which the new roots on the offsets could grow.

Today manure is difficult to acquire for those living in towns, except for spent mushroom compost which has lime in it. As the auricula seems indifferent to lime, this is an excellent substitute. Care must always be taken that the manure is well rotted, as fresh manure contains ammonia and can burn the roots, killing the plants. Cats and dogs are also a hazard in this respect, and I know of one garden where the newly-dug ground is always covered with rose, holly or other prickly prunings!

A few years ago some border auricula seedlings were supplied to the Castle Bromwich Garden Trust, near Birmingham, that is restoring an old garden to its 1730 state. They wanted 'old-fashioned' plants to give the garden authenticity and 'rejects' from a double breeding programme – plants that looked similar to those painted by Redouté – were deemed admissible. Apparently they are to be provided with manure from the Birmingham Police stables, the acme of luxury for an auricula. (The garden is expected to be opened to the public by the time this book is published.) Border auriculas are grown in many other famous gardens, such as Wisley and Harlow Car, while John Treasure's lovely garden at Burford, Shropshire, has a 'private' round enclave. From a distance a large clump of 'Yellow Dusty Millers', a lovely sight in April, can be observed growing there.

There are always classes for border auriculas in the Auricula Societies' shows. They are judged for effect, sturdiness, attractive strong leaves, mealiness and flowers of a rich bright colour held on a long, strong stem. Many have that powdering of farina around the eye of the flower that adds so much to their charms, and some are attractively ruffed or fluted. The flowers may be 'pin-eyed' or 'thrum-eyed'. when the pants grow in a garden this factor is of little relevance and unnoticeable, but the trusses must be clear of the foliage without any need for staking. Some competitors do temporarily stake their borders for the journey to the shows, taking care to remove them before staging. Any plants with the stakes remaining would be disqualified.

One thing that borders are not judged for, regrettably, is their marvellous perfume. To enter a greenhouse full of flowering auriculas can be a delight for the perfume alone. A strong clump of border auriculas can be picked for flower arrangement and the perfume enjoyed indoors. Because the other auricula sections are judged on form and appearance, perfume is seen as a secondary feature even with borders.

Borders are often said to be very old plants, and some are reputed to have been growing in the same garden for 100 years or more. This may or may not be true but undoubtedly a few *are* very old. Gwen Baker was once given a plant that had been growing in the garden of the donor's aunt for twenty years. It had a lovely yellow flower that was visible from a distance, and it has been named 'Aunt Laura'. There are a number of attractive plants that have been selected by nurserymen and sold under the name of their nursery, like 'Paradise Yellow', named after the Paradise

Plant Centre in Southern England. As these plants are grown by non-specialists they are almost always borders for general garden decoration.

List of Varieties

Some of the names that follow are taken from plants exhibited at shows, some grown by the authors; others have been suggested by fellow growers; and the remainder are from *The Plant Finder*. The list can never be exhaustive as new varieties arrive every year.

Beeches Challenger (L. Wigley, 1978, 'Old Royal Blue Dusty Miller' x 'Windward Blue') The raiser states 'an outstanding seedling with all the vigour of its seed parent plus the refinement of 'Windward Blue''. It produces large heads of rich blue, white-centred flowers on strong stems above mealed foliage. This plant has won a number of Premiers at the London show but offsets slowly, so has not been widely distributed.

Bellamy Pride (B. Walker, *c.* 1985) Sumptuous white-flowered truss over lightly farinose leaves. Thrum-eye. Given an Award of Merit on its first showing at Solihull. Although shown in the border classes, it is usually grown in a pot. The flowers have a slight blueish tinge.

Blue Velvet The flowers are deep purple-blue, round and velvety, with a cream centre that fades white, freely produced, while the leaves are plain green. The nearest to a true blue auricula, pleasantly scented.

Broadwell Gold Now an old variety, with lightly-dusted leaves and big, flat golden-yellow flowers, borne on long, strong stems soon making a big clump. Premier Border, Midland Auricula Show 1990.

Bramley Rose (I. Hawthorn, commercial seed) A strong-growing plant with tall stem and rosy red flowers, it has a stained eye and a smattering of meal.

Chamois (J. Mercer, 'Rufus' x border cross) A strong-growing variety, with petals the colour of soft leather. The flowers are pin-eyed and freely produced. The leaves are meal-free. A 'halfway house' plant on the borderline between *P.* x *pubescens* and a normal border auricula.

Craig Nordie Dark-red flowers with a star-like pentagonal centre and paddle-shaped, mealy leaves. Found by A. Duguid near Deeside in the 1940s. Very rare.

Duke of Edinburgh A favourite plant of Margery Fish, well described in her book *Cottage Garden Flowers*, with brick-red cream-centred flowers over pointed, powdered leaves. Beginning to show signs of age.

Dusky Yellow Offsets freely, bearing large umbels of mustard-yellow frilly flowers, over grey leaves, and multiplies rapidly. Several different plants masquerade under this name and it is difficult to know which – if any – are the 'true' plant.

Frittenden Yellow A strong-growing plant with mealy leaves and bright yellow, thrum-eyed flowers, similar to 'Broadwell Gold', but neither as fine nor as easy to grow.

George Edge A yellow-flowered variety found in an old garden.

George Harrison A pale-whitish flower with lightly mealed leaves. Grown by a Scottish nursery, it may have originated with Mrs McMurtrie, a well-known grower of old-fashioned plants.

George Swinnerton's Leathercoat See Leathercoat.

Kate Haywood A strong-growing plant with pale-green, lightly mealed leaves, and creamy pale-yellow flowers. Raised by the late Ralph Haywood when he worked at Joe Elliot's Broadwell Nursery, and named after his wife. A good plant which sets seed readily and produces good offspring.

Lady Lowther Primrose-yellow frilly flowers over lightly farinose leaves. Pin-eyed, sweet scented, does well in open ground.

Leathercoat A very old variety, discovered by the auricula historian, Ruth Duthie, growing at Filkins, Oxfordshire; now feeble and rare. Pinkish-brown flowers provide an original contrast to the more usual flower shades.

Linnet Praised by Roy Genders, who thought it lost to cultivation in the 1950s. Named after the bird, the flowers are variously described either as fawn and primrose or as mustard-brown and green.

Lintz Lawrence Wigley discovered this plant in an old nurseryman's frame in Wallington, Surrey, around 1958. Its origin is unknown but it has proved a reliable grower, winning several awards at the London shows. Now less vigorous, at its peak it carried large heads of velvety-brown flowers with a creamy centre and distinctive perfume.

Lockyers Gem (W. Lockyer, 1989, unnamed violet x 'Paradise Yellow') One of the best of recently-raised borders and a 'breakthrough', as it is a distinctly striped form, large but neat purple flowers flecked and striped with cream.

Magnolia Doubles as a border and a *pubescens* hybrid. Small leaves but strongly-growing, it has numerous heads of magnolia-grey flowers.

McWatts Blue Mealy leaves, grey-blue shaded flowers, becoming darker as they age. Tends to flop over. It has a sweet scent. A favourite, especially in the garden. Named for Dr McWatt, author of *Primulas of Europe* (1923).

Mrs Harris A big-flowered plant, found originally in the garden of an old lady. Creamy-white pips, strong grower. Seems identical to a plant sold by Edrom Nurseries as 'Rob Dalgleish'; they may be the same.

Mrs Lowry A connoisseur's plant, again found in an old garden and somewhat feeble now, but choice, well-formed purple blue flowers over lightly-farinose foliage. A good parent.

Old Gold Dusty Miller A rare plant with small leaves, whiter with farina than any other known, and golden-yellow pips. Most attractive. Introduced by one of the greatest growers of old-fashioned primulas, Mrs Mary McMurtrie, of Balbithan, Aberdeenshire.

Old Irish Blue Several plants, some impostors, bear this name. The true plant has a long thin carrot and blue-shaded frilly flowers, with a white centre over meal-free plain-green leaves.

Old Irish Scented Originated at Lissadell Gardens, near Sligo. It has neat, rounded, light-mustard coloured pips. Pleasantly scented, though no more so than other border auriculas.

Old Red Dusty Miller There are at least two varieties with this name. One has ragged petals and a crimson colour, the other has entire petals and is bright red. Both have mealy leaves.

Old Suffolk Bronze Its flowers are browny-yellow, over green leaves. An old variety, discovered by Roy Genders in a Suffolk cottage garden. It may have been over-praised but it remains an interesting auricula with unusual colour.

Old Yellow Dusty Miller As its name suggests, it has yellow flowers and attractive leaves dusted with farina. The flowers are often trumpet-shaped. A tough old timer, grows into good clumps. There is more than one variety bearing this name.

Osbourne Green Discovered over fifty years ago in an Irish garden by the legendary Miss Wynn of Avoca, who believed it had grown there for over 200 years. Its leaves are meal-free and its purple flowers green-tipped. At one time reduced to a single plant, it now appears safe in cultivation. There have been suggestions that this plant is in fact an early

edged auricula, although the original name has been lost.

Paradise Yellow Bears clusters of rather tubular pips, bright-yellow, thrum-eyed pips freely borne, over meal-free leaves. A vigorous variety. Introduced and named by the Paradise Plant Nursery.

Queen Alexandra Presumed to have been raised in Edwardian times in Northern Ireland. The flowers are pale-primrose, pin-eyed, freely borne over green foliage and are strongly fragrant. Several different plants masquerade under this name.

Redstart Is listed in *The Plant Finder* as a border, but the only plant known under this name is a fancy auricula.

Royal Velvet A strong grower with light-green leaves and large trusses of rich, velvety crimson-purple flowers with a cream centre and throat.

Rufus Flowers of an unusual brick-red shade in large trusses over green foliage. Its eye has a characteristic red stain arching in from the petals. Can be grown in a scree bed, as well as in pots for show. Some growers would classify 'Rufus' more appropriately as a large *pubescens*-type hybrid.

Rusty Red A most unusual and striking colour, with a stained eye and lots of personality, perhaps the best of recently-raised garden auriculas. We hope that it will eventually become widely distributed. From Mr Bowen of Llanelli.

Saint Gerrard's White This is a scarce plant with crumpled whitish flowers and a deeper eye.

St Martins (L. Wigley, 1971, 'Old Gold' x 'Yellow Dusty Miller') The raiser states 'for some years this proved a very satisfactory plant with attractively mealed foliage and heads of nicely scented rusty-yellow flowers.' It was shown successfully in London on several occasions. Its vigour declined during the early 1980s.

White Witch Raised by Bob Archdale from seed obtained from the Alpine Garden Society. Whitish flowers with a slight yellow-pink tinge. The flowers are small but produced in huge quantities. Possibly due to this it lacks vigour, literally 'flowering itself to death'.

Wycliffe Harmony A 'Rufus' x yellow border seedling like 'Chamois'. Very similar in colour and form, perhaps more yellow, with a flower that flattens more. The pips are thrum-eyed and it has green leaves. As yet of limited distribution.

6 Cultivation

PROTECTION

Auriculas are hardy perennials and may be grown successfully in the open, enduring severe weather without difficulty. Florists' auriculas are almost invariably grown in pots under glass during winter and spring to protect the flowers and foliage from wind and rain. Show auriculas, especially the heavily-mealed varieties, are particularly susceptible and one drop of rain can mark the foliage or cause the paste of the flower to 'run'. Another problem is bees, particularly large bumble bees, which are attracted to the flowers, ruining the paste; they must be excluded from the greenhouse, especially if you wish to exhibit plants. Green mesh netting gives adequate protection and can be arranged to cover all vents and hang like a curtain over open doors. It is also useful for providing shade.

It was common in the past for plants to be grown in frames, or tall glass jars with the base removed – these were manufactured for the textile trade. Today's growers would normally keep their plants in a greenhouse during winter and spring, moving them to frames, if available, during the hot summer months.

The ideal greenhouse is the 'Alpine house' used by specialists in alpine plants. These structures benefit from having continuous ventilators along both sides and in the roof. Some also have bottom ventilators controlled by sliding wooden or metal panels. Unfortunately, they are considerably more expensive than normal greenhouses and thus unavailable to many people. Many other types of greenhouse are available and are perfectly satisfactory, providing that additional ventilation panels are installed. Most companies that sell greenhouses will provide extra vents for a small additional cost and some growers have greenhouses with doors at each end which, when open, allow air to circulate freely. Both aluminium and wooden greenhouses are suitable. Heating is not necessary for auriculas, so there are no fuel bills.

It is wise to obtain the largest greenhouse that finances allow. Space soon becomes a premium, and smaller houses are difficult to keep cool and properly ventilated. Flowering plants need plenty of room, especially those with mealed foliage.

The usual advice on siting a greenhouse is that it should run north/south and be free from overhanging trees. An east/west greenhouse is only acceptable if the south-facing side is shaded by a tree or building. Auriculas prefer shade in summer and many successful growers utilize natural shade to keep the plants cool and contented. 'For example,' writes Peter Ward, 'my greenhouse at Yarnton near Oxford was shaded by an apple tree. When I moved to Solihull the same Alton [greenhouse] was sited under a large oak, while at Saltford it was beneath a willow. Gwen has two greenhouses in her Wolverhampton garden that benefit from the shade of small deciduous trees. Of course dense shade, such as that from conifers, is to be avoided.' Auriculas and most primulas flower before the trees mentioned have their new leaves. When the leaves develop the house becomes shaded and keeps much cooler as the hottest period of the year approaches. In theory the plants could become drawn but with broken shade, particularly if the north side is not obscured, this is not a problem. Natural shade is superior to other methods of shading except perhaps for slatted, wooden roll-up blinds.

If one has to resort to artificial shading, the best alternative is green mesh netting, either Netlon, Rokelene or similar, available from garden centres. With wooden greenhouses this is easily attached using drawing pins. Metal greenhouses make this more difficult but garden centres sell a variety of plastic clips and accessories that enable you to fix the netting. Painted-on shading, for instance Coolglass, is inexpensive and easy to apply but is at a disadvantage in cloudy conditions. For those whose budget allows, there is a number of different types of roller blinds that can be fitted to the outside of the grrenhouse, suspended from the roof beams. Some of the old growers used old lace curtains, and the famous Halifax grower of the 1950s, Lewis Ambler, used an old carpet to shade the roof of his small home-made greenhouse! In any event, shading should be in place by the end of March and removed at the beginning of September. James Douglas of Great Bookham stated in his 1934 lecture to the RHS: 'Using a medium fabric, we shade between 11 am and 5 pm (new time) from the 1st April to the 1st September'. If you use the green mesh netting, it is necessary to increase the number of layers as the strength of the sun increases.

Solid benches are preferred, with the plants standing on a layer of sand or gravel or even 'Hortag' granules. This provides additional drainage, absorbs surplus moisture and keeps the plants cool in summer as the moisture in the plunge material evaporates. Slatted benches are unsuitable: small pots tend to fall over. If such benches are used, the plants should stand on trays filled with sand or gravel.

During the summer a greenhouse is not the best place for auriculas as they detest hot, dry conditions. After flowering in early May they should be moved to a north-facing frame, protected from the midday sun and normally kept open. This is the ideal that may not always be possible; many growers will have to make do with more makeshift arrangements, especially in the tiny gardens that are a feature of modern housing estates.

Frames are not as convenient as greenhouses, but they can usually be raised to enable easier access to the plants. This also makes it more difficult for crawling pests to attack them. If the frames stand on legs they can be protected by, for example, grease bands or glue from a Trapitt tube. Once again, the plants should stand on a layer of sand or gravel. If the frame is at ground level the plunge mix should be laid over a sheet of polythene to prevent worms entering the pots from below.

The cultivation of border auriculas is not covered in this chapter because they are not generally pot-grown plants. For information on their cultivation see Chapter 5.

COMPOSTS

This topic has always generated controversy and much has been written on the subject during the auricula's history. The well-known growers in the early part of last century, Emmerton, Hogg and Maddock, used the most extraordinary mixtures containing animal manures, bullocks' blood and various other noxious substances, including night soil. Later it was realized such concoctions were unnecessary: the plant can be grown perfectly well on a simple diet.

James Douglas, in his 1934 lecture to the RHS, described some of these early composts as 'fearsome concoctions' and went on to say:

> There are, of course, many different composts used today. I have had experience with one only, a mixture that has been in use at Edenside for the last forty-five years; it is composed of the following easily-procured ingredients:
>
> 1 barrow-load of fibrous loam torn into small pieces;
> 1 barrow-load of two-year old leaves riddled through a half-inch sieve;
> 1 barrow-load of rotted horse manure, also riddled.
>
> To every barrow-load of compost add one 5 in (12.7 cm) pot of bone meal, one 5 in (12.7 cm) pot of coarse sand, and one 5 in (12.7 cm) pot of crushed oyster shell.
>
> Nothing else has been used to my knowledge in the cultivation of the auricula at Edenside. People have hinted that there are secrets known only to experts. There are no secrets and no mysterious preparations. All that is necessary to ensure success in the cultivation of the Florist's auricula is fresh air, good loam, and common sense.

It should be noted that today a substantial body of opinion still holds that special composts are quite unnecessary for pot-grown auriculas. Allan Hawkes, for example, buys 'the cheapest local source of John Innes No. 2' and considers that the results are very similar to those he gained when he used special mixes. David Hadfield holds similar views, again using locally-bought John Innes, modified by adding leaf mould and grit.

Despite the availability of ready-made composts, particularly the loam-based John Innes and the soilless UCL types, some auricula growers still continue to make their own compost.

Possibly the most highly regarded post-war grower was Fred Buckley and those who saw his plants were unstinting in their praise. Dr D. A. Duthie, a very good grower in his own right, told one author about his first sight of Buckley's plants. Dr Duthie stepped into the greenhouse and was stunned by the floral display. There were hundreds of plants flowering to a standard that would have given many of them Premier awards at any show. Buckley was very fastidious, and this included his compost mix:

> Top spit turfy loam, pulled into small pieces from half-size downwards, without riddling into a finer state.
> *Shows*: 3 buckets loam; 2 buckets leaf mould; 1 bucket grit; 1 60-pot bone meal; 2 60-pot charcoal; 1$\frac{1}{2}$ 60-pot oyster shell.
> *Alpines*: 2 buckets loam; 1 bucket leaf mould; $\frac{1}{2}$ bucket grit; 1 60-pot bone meal; 1 60-pot charcoal; 1 60-pot oyster shell.

This is the mixture quoted under 'Macclesfield' in Part 1 of the 1959 Northern yearbook, 'Macclesfield' being Buckley. The buckets would have been 2 gal (9 litres) and the '60-pot' referred to could be one of three sizes, but was almost certainly the 3 in (7.62 cm) pot. It will be noted that he even went to the extent of preparing different mixtures for shows and alpines. No present grower does this, nor indeed did any of Buckley's contemporaries, many of whose mixtures were listed in the same 1959 article. Buckley used Kettering loam, as did many others, because at the time it was still readily available and famous among enthusiasts. Today good loam is scarce and has been for some years, but unsterilized shredded loam can be obtained from several John Innes manufacturers. Unless you can obtain a good quality loam from a reliable source it is preferable to stick to John Innes or an equivalent loam-based, sterilized compost. Under no circumstances use soil dug from the garden for pot-grown auriculas.

Before sterilized composts arrived, normal practice was to have a 'loam stack'. This was composed of top-spit turfy loam dug from a meadow or field that had been well grazed by animals. The pieces of turf were stacked upside down with cow manure between each layer. The stack would be covered to keep off excessive rain and left to mature for up to three years. When ready, with the grasses fully decomposed, a spade was used to chop the matured loam from top to bottom. Only the amount immediately required was removed and the stack might last for some years.

Leaf mould has fallen out of fashion because it is difficult to obtain and variable in quality. Peat, which has replaced leaf mould, is becoming less acceptable on environmental grounds and other substitutes such as coir (coconut fibre) are being advocated to replace it. Many auricula growers remain unconvinced about the merits of peat, which has no nutrient value, and believe a good oak- or beech-leaf mould far superior. The leaf mould should be three-year-old half rotted leaves, riddled and crushed into small pieces. When ready for use the leaves crumble to the touch. The coarser, less decayed pieces are put over the crocks, pieces of broken pot or Hortag granules, in the bottom of the pot. It is noticeable, when repotting, that plant roots search out these partly decayed leaves, some-

thing that does not happen with peat. The difficulty is that removing leaves from beech and oak woods is frowned upon and frequently illegal. Quite acceptable leaf mould can be made from other types of leaves but beech and oak are preferred because they rot down more slowly.

If peat is used as a substitute for leaf mould, a good coarse moss peat is preferred. One drawback is its inability to take up moisture when dry: water runs off. A type of peat known as Sorbex was once available, imported from Germany. This was much favoured by alpine plant enthusiasts on the grounds that, as a very soft peat, it would absorb moisture when dust dry. We are unaware of a current source, but Russian peat has occasionally been available and is a very similar product.

Derek Telford, the leading Northern grower of Alpine auriculas, uses the following mix:

1 freshly-made bag of Bentley's John Innes No. 2 (approx. 13 kg)
2 gal (9 litres) of grated peat
2 gal (9 litres) of sharp granite chippings
8 in (20 cm) pot of well-grated, well-rotted cow manure
5 in (13 cm) pot of grated charcoal
8 oz (226 grams) of J.I. base fertilizer and 3 oz (85 grams) of Dolomite lime to each bushel

A $\frac{1}{4}$ in (6 mm) riddle is used to rid the compost of large lumps of peat, cow manure and charcoal. Derek had previously used molehill soil collected from a local field but found the task increasingly onerous and has now opted for the mix given above.

Peter Ward has used a compost based on Buckley's for some years, replacing some of the ingredients due to unavailability. The mix is:

Three buckets (27 litres) unsterilized loam
Two buckets (18 litres) half-rotted oak- or beech-leaf mould
One bucket (9 litres) Cornish grit

1. 'Dr Duthie' *(top right)*

2. 'Jupiter' *(top left)*

3. 'Fleminghouse' *(bottom left)*

4. 'Roberto' *(bottom right)*

5. 'Prague' *(opposite top left)*

6. 'Chloe' *(opposite top right)*

7. 'Gavin Ward' *(opposite middle right)*

8. Seedling 'Gavin Ward x Warwick'
   (opposite bottom left)

9. 'Clare' *(top left)*

10. 'Warwick' *(middle left)*

11. 'Grey Hawk' *(top right)*

12. 'Margaret Martin' *(bottom right)*

13. 'The Bride' *(top left)*

14. 'Sharmans Cross' *(middle left)*

15. 'Brookfield' *(bottom left)*

16. 'Prince John' *(opposite top)*

17. 'Gay Crusader' *(opposite bottom)*

18. Pink Seedling *(top right)*

19. 'Mark' *(middle right)*

20. 'Blossom' *(opposite top)*

21. 'John Wayne'
    (opposite bottom)

22. 'Janie Hill' *(top)*

23. 'Bolero' *(bottom)*

24. 'Adrian' *(top)*

25. 'Valerie' *(bottom left)*

26. 'Verdi' *(opposite top)*

27. 'Beckminster' *(opposite bottom left)*

28. 'Sirius' *(opposite bottom right)*

29. 'Lee Paul' *(top right)*

30. 'Sandra' *(left)*

31. 'Mikado' *(top left)*

32. 'Remus' *(middle right)*

33. 'Tracy Ward'
(opposite top left)

34. 'April Moon'
(opposite top right)

35. 'Brompton'
(bottom right)

36. 'Upton Belle'
(middle left)

37. 'Moonglow'
(middle bottom)

38. 'Cherry' *(opposite top left)*

39. 'Golden Chartreuse' *(opposite top right)*

40. 'Diamond' *(opposite middle right)*

41. 'Westcott Pride' *(opposite bottom right)*

42. 'Koh-i-noor' *(opposite bottom left)*

43. 'Thirlmere' *(top left)*

44. 'Gaia' *(top right)*

45. Seedling double auriculas *(above)*

46. 'Jane Myers' *(bottom right)*

47. 'Susannah' *(top left)*

48. 'Pink Fondant' *(top right)*

49. 'Gingernut' *(bottom left)*

50. 'Sarah Brightman' *(middle right)*

51. **'Raleigh Stripe'** *(top left)*

52. **'May Tiger'** *(top middle)*

53. Yellow ground fancy show auricula *(top right)*

54. **'Spaceage'** *(bottom right)*

55. Seedling border auricula *(middle left)*

56. **'Bellamy Pride'** *(top left)*

57. **'Rusty Red'** *(top right)*

58. Red garden auricula *(middle left)*

59. Seedling border *(middle right)*

60. Borders on show bench, **'Mrs Harris'** at centre *(bottom left)*

One 3 in (7.62 cm) pot oyster shell
One 3 in (7.62 cm) pot crushed charcoal
One 3 in (7.62 cm) pot seaweed powder
12 oz (340 grams) Vitax Q4

If leaf mould is unavailable this is replaced by a 50/50 mixture of moss peat (or Russian peat) and Cambark Fine Grade, a specially-formulated and composted bark made for potting composts. The bucket is a 2 gallon- (9 litre-) capacity one, and it is essential that the whole compost is very well mixed. The compost is prepared two to three months before use.

If one does not want to go to the extreme of mixing one's own compost, a good quality John Innes, preferably with grit or sharp sand added, will produce satisfactory results. While many feel that special mixtures are unnecessary, John Innes composts are very variable, depending on the ingredients used, especially the loam. No two ever seem to be the same, though they are supposed to be identical. For potting they are produced in three grades, Nos 1, 2 and 3. Grade 1 has 4 oz (113 g) of John Innes base fertilizer per 8 gal (36 litres), Grade 2 has 8 oz (226 g) and Grade 3 has 12 oz (339 g). Without modification Grade 2 is the most suitable and most commonly used. Another crucial point is freshness, as ammonia build up occurs in old unused bags and may kill plants when it is used for potting. There is a John Innes Producers' Association in the UK and members have the logo on the bags of compost. This Association was formed to provide a guarantee that members' products would be of the required specification and quality. Unfortunately, problems arose over this very issue of standardisation and some companies, who in the authors' experience produce very acceptable J.I., have now left the Association. If John Innes is used we would advocate some modification before use, even for clay pots. Contrary to some

published information this is not detrimental. We would suggest the following:

three or four parts J.I. No. 3
one part peat, or Cambark Fine Grade or moss peat
one part grit.

It is important to ensure that this is very well mixed. This is approximately the mix that Gwen Baker also uses for plastic pots. The composts above are for clay pots, except that of Derek Telford, who uses $3\frac{1}{2}$ in (8.89 cm) plastic pots. When plastic pots are used, it is necessary to modify the compost by adding grit. The amount or percentage of grit used depends on the texture of the compost; if heavy add more, if lighter add less. This will be discussed later.

Earlier we mentioned peat-based composts, of which many are available. They originated at the University of California and have a peat base with added nutrients; most have a wetting agent to make for easier watering. Since then, several variants have been introduced that include peat/sand and peat/perlite mixes, and some with a small amount of sterilized loam. These peat composts are not suitable for growing auriculas in clay pots and this should be avoided. Good plants can be grown in peat-based compost in plastic pots and some growers succeed in producing plants that are equal to those grown in clays. With this type of compost the nutrients only last for about six weeks, so subsequent liquid feeding is essential.

POTS

Auriculas can be grown successfully in both plastic and clay pots. Each pot has its advocates. Many of the leading growers still use clays and consider that better plants result, but the use of plastics is increasing: they are both cheaper and more readily obtainable.

Only two sizes of clay or plastic pot are needed: 3 in (7.62 cm) and $3\frac{1}{2}$ in (8.89 cm). The preferred clay is the 'long tom', which is deeper than the normal pot. It has been said by other writers that some plants need a 4 in (10 cm) pot but this is unnecessary; $3\frac{1}{2}$ in (8.89 cm) is quite large enough. The reason for using the long tom is the tendency of some varieties to grow out of the pot. The carrot or stem elongates and may be 2 in (5 cm) or so above soil level. Once again a number of experienced growers question the necessity for long toms, believing that the plants grow as well in ordinary pots.

Long tom pots are not always readily obtainable and for some years, after Sankeys and Wards ceased production around 1968, they could not be found. It was soon discovered that plastic pots were not entirely suitable for some plants and a few small concerns were started up, often by a single person, producing hand-fired frost-proof pots. Initially only 5 in (12.7 cm) long toms were made, for growing clematis. Following requests from auricula growers, sizes approximating to $3\frac{1}{2}$ in (8.89 cm) were produced. A long tom can cost £1 or more, making it an expensive purchase. Some of these small firms will make batches to order, but check the cost first.

Clay pots have several disadvantages. They are heavy and because of their porous nature can get very dirty. This takes the form of a greenish slime, with a lime encrustation in hard-water areas. Cleaning them regularly, using warm water and a sponge cloth, will keep this under control.

Cleaning the pots prior to repotting is a major exercise that involves soaking them in water for several days and then scrubbing them with Brillo pads or a wire brush. Derek Telford (who now uses plastic pots) recommends two Steradent tablets placed in a 2-gal (9-litre) bucket of water, in which the pots

are immersed. After a few hours the deposits are easily removed by wiping. Others have suggested using Biotex and kettle-descaling liquids.

The procedure for cleaning pots in early spring is as follows: prepare a bowl of warm water and add a few drops of Jeyes fluid. Using a kitchen sponge cloth, carefully wipe the pots, slowly in order to avoid specks of grime from the pot marking the plant leaves. As the pots may be very slimy, be careful that they do not slip from your hand. Apart from easing the handling of your plants, you should not put a plant on the show bench in a dirty pot. It is difficult to remove some of the lime encrustation that stains the pots; sandpaper may help, as may scouring pads. This is an annoying feature of clay pots, particularly well-used ones. During the cleaning operation one advantage of plastic pots becomes obvious: watering is required more frequently with clay pots and can be a problem in hot weather. It is even more of a problem if one is absent on holiday for more than a few days. Plunging the pots in sand or a peat and sand mixture is one solution, commonly practised by growers of Alpine plants. In support of clay pots, the dangers of overwatering are less great than with plastic pots.

The claimed benefits of the plastic pot are fourfold: watering is much reduced, they are easy to clean, weigh very little and are cheaper than clays. The benefit of reduced watering is not always the advantage it seems. Overwatering allied to a heavy, poorly-drained compost can very easily cause root rot. Clay pots dry out quickly, so careless watering is not so crucial, especially if the busy grower has little time. If loam-based compost is used with a plastic pot the addition of grit, 30 to 50 per cent by bulk, may be needed. The actual amount will depend on the texture of the compost. This reduces the amount of fertilizer available to the plant, and a weak liquid feed of approximately quarter strength should be given regularly when watering.

In summer, heat is the enemy of the auricula, especially in a very dry atmosphere. The compost in plastic pots becomes much warmer than that in clays and keeping the plants cool is very important. Plunging or part-plunging in sand or peat is one way of doing this: both clay and plastic pots are cooled as the water in the plunge material evaporates. It is common to find roots growing out of the bottom of the pot into the plunge material, especially in plastics with their larger number of drainage holes. However, the plunge material should not be allowed to remain saturated with water all the time. Attempts to utilize capillary watering for auriculas have in the past led to disaster, although at least one modern grower does so successfully. Another possible pitfall of plastic pots is the difference in capacity between the thin-walled plastic pot and the thick-walled clay. A $3\frac{1}{2}$ in (8.89 cm) plastic pot holds considerably more compost than the equivalent clay. (This is relative to all other sizes.) An important rule in growing auriculas is not to overpot them. In addition, many plants seem to flower better if they are slightly pot-bound.

REPOTTING

Repotting is an annual task for auricula growers. It provides the plants with a fresh supply of compost, allows inspection of the roots and carrot, and enables offsets to be removed more easily. The most contentious point is when it should take place. The options are immediately after flowering in late May, or mid- to late August, possibly running into early September. There is no consensus among growers about which is best. One theory is that early repotting gives the plants

a longer period to recover and better flowering results. Those who do it later argue that newly-potted plants are seriously at risk during the hot summer months. Growers in the south of England face more trying conditions during the summer and many favour August. If August is hot, this operation may be deferred to early September. Peter Ward changed to late repotting over twenty years ago after severe losses during the summer; while Gwen Baker made the same move following heavy losses from vine weevil grubs. After practising late repotting for many years we are convinced that it is the best option, but not everyone agrees. David Hadfield in Lancashire and Martin Sheader in Southampton both repot as soon as possible after flowering, and with excellent results.

An alternative method, mostly for show auriculas, is to cut the tops off three-year-old plants after flowering; the tops are then discarded. Peter Ward writes:

The system I use does not involve much orthodox repotting although some of the plants are dealt with in this way. Some years ago on a trip to London I overheard Dr D. A. Duthie gently reprimanding a well-known Midland grower ... for having many plants in his collection over eight years old. Duthie was making the point that [he] was not renewing his plants often enough. The older an auricula becomes the more susceptible it is to carrot rot. The carrot thickens as the plant ages and the condition called 'canker', or hard rot of the carrot, may occur. The flowering performance of these veterans declines and they become passengers. Instead of repotting, up to two-thirds of the plants are decapitated at soil level using a very sharp knife or scalpel. This is done immediately after flowering and the plants placed to one side of the greenhouse. Most have at least one new shoot growing already and soon afterwards others appear. Some varieties do not respond so well to this treatment and should be repotted by more orthodox methods. If no offsets are visible then I would not recommend doing it.

For normal repotting the procedure is as follows: the plants are allowed to become fairly dry so that the soil is easily removed. They are carefully knocked out of their pots: hold the pot upside down and tap it on the bench. Be careful not to break the pot when doing so. Plants come out of plastic pots readily if the sides are squeezed first. Most of the soil is removed from the roots by gentle pressure

and shaking. Some growers then wash the remainder of the soil from the roots in a bowl or bucket of water. Any rooted offsets are removed, together with any dead or unhealthy-looking roots. The carrot will be examined for signs of decay and may be shortened depending on its condition.

Sometimes half or more will be removed, taking most of the old roots. If most of the roots are removed, a much smaller pot should be used, even if the plant has large leaves. In order to keep the plant to a single crown any small buds should be rubbed out. A long carrot, even though healthy, may need to be shortened if most of the roots grow from the top part. This is done with a sharp knife or scalpel, sterilized in a suitable solution after cutting each plant. Sterilization guards

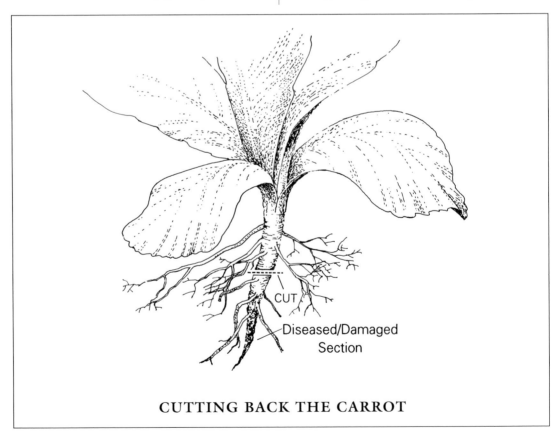

CUTTING BACK THE CARROT

against the spread of virus. Where offsets are removed the wound is covered with a mixture of flowers of sulphur or powdered charcoal. This is also done to the cut end of the carrot. If root aphis is found, the roots should be dipped in a dilute solution of one of the proprietary insecticides, but be sure to wear rubber gloves when doing this. By far the best answer is to treat the plants with a systemic insecticide two weeks before repotting. You can repot immediately (the authors prefer to do this), or let the wounds dry first (which is favoured by others). The wounds are allowed to dry so that they can callus, making them less likely to rot. The disadvantage is that the roots also dry out, which is less desirable.

If you use clays, before commencing this operation have ready a supply of crocks, Hortag or Perlag granules for drainage, fresh compost, clean pots, plant labels, marker pens, and knives. Crocks are pieces of broken pot collected and perhaps shaped over several years to fit the bottom of the pot. Hortag granules can be bought at garden centres and are now in common use. Some growers think this type of drainage unnecessary with a porous compost and have stopped using either.

Prior to repotting, soak the clay pots in a bucket of clean water for several hours. If the pots are used dry, they will absorb moisture very quickly and the newly-potted plant will dry out. Remove the pots from the bucket and allow them to surface dry. Place the crocks or granules carefully over the drainage hole, which can be covered by a small piece of mesh to keep worms out – needed particularly if the plants are grown in frames. A small amount of compost is poured into the pot over the crocks, which can have some coarse leaves or fibrous pieces of peat covering them. Then hold the plant centrally in the pot and

pour compost around the roots to within $\frac{1}{2}$ in (1 cm) of the top. The pot should be tapped on the bench several times during this process to firm the soil. Strong finger pressure is all that is needed, and ramming is inadvisable as it can damage the roots. It is normal practice to repot all the plants of one variety together, so that small offsets can be potted together. It also avoids the possibility of plants being wrongly labelled.

The best way to water clay pots is by immersion and this should be done immediately, standing the pots in trays of water up to two-thirds depth. Some growers will mix a fungicide with the water; others may add an insecticide. The plants should be kept shaded and as cool as possible for the next few weeks until new roots develop. On warm evenings a cool mist spray of water is beneficial. If possible, watering should be withheld for up to four weeks. Be very careful with watering and if in doubt leave the plants for a few more days. The leaves may remain limp for some time until new roots develop. A moisture meter can be a useful tool, but as they have bulky probes take care when using them.

When using plastic pots, the procedure changes. The compost needs to be more porous. Sharp grit should be added and well mixed, the amount varying from a quarter to a half by bulk. This ensures that the compost drains freely so that the plant is not waterlogged. In plastic pots the compost should be lightly firmed, whether using a modified John Innes or a peat-based compost. Hortag granules can be put in the bottom of the pot to help drainage if required. The level of the compost in both clay and plastics should be at least $\frac{1}{2}$ in (1 cm) below the rim. Watering can be by immersion but not to the same extent as with clays. Some growers prefer to water in the normal fashion.

PROPAGATION

Multiplying the plants by the taking of offsets is the usual way of propagating auriculas and the only way of increasing named varieties until recently. Offsets are miniature plants that grow from latent buds on the carrot. In recent years micropropagation has been introduced, a laboratory based method that is mainly confined to large commercial concerns. Auriculas are being produced by this method in a limited number of varieties.

The number of offsets produced by most plants annually varies from one to four on most show auriculas, but can be considerably greater on some of the Alpines and doubles. If the number of small offset buds is excessive the surplus can be removed by rubbing them off with the fingers. Taking them i.e. removing, potting up and labelling separately is a fairly simple operation and is normally done when the plant is repotted. You can of course take offsets as soon as the plants start into growth early in the year. If the plants are required for showing this is not recommended. Most offsets will have some roots and grow away without difficulty. Unrooted offsets can easily be rooted provided they have a reasonable stem. The normal compost with an equal amount of sharp sand added is suitable. You can also root them in sharp sand or perlite or even peat compost. Pot them into small 2 in (5 cm) or $2\frac{1}{2}$ in (6.35 cm) plastic pots singly, or three or four round the sides of a 3 in (7.62 cm) pot. Make sure they are firm, the compost moist but not saturated and keep well shaded and cool. They can be put in a propagator with a clear plastic top, with the vents open. This, however, is not essential and they will root without being covered at all. Heat is not necessary but good ventilation is to prevent botrytis. In three to four weeks the majority will be rooted. When

this is obvious and growth is restarting they should be potted on into the normal compost with perhaps a little extra sand or grit. When the roots fill the pot they can be potted on, using the normal compost, into larger pots.

The type of offset produced by different varieties varies. Some, like the show varieties 'Clare' and 'Warwick' and the border variety 'Old Irish Blue', produce what are called suckers. These are offsets that grow from near the bottom of the carrot and have long thin stems well provided with roots. They are easy to remove, often with a gentle tug, and grow on when repotted without obvious check. The wound on the carrot is insignificant and can be dusted with sulphur, chalk, powdered charcoal or brushed with methylated spirits. Flowers of sulphur is a mild fungicide obtainable from most garden centres in the yellow form. Many Alpines, doubles and borders produce rooted offsets freely, those at or below soil level usually develop good roots. Some varieties present more of a problem; usually those with a short thick carrot. The few offsets have short thick stems themselves and grow from higher on the carrot. They may be unrooted or have only one or two short roots. In such cases they may have to be removed using a knife or scalpel, carefully cutting through the base where they join the parent plant. A large clean wound results and must be treated with the sulphur or charcoal mixture. These are the most difficult offsets to root and a very large wound on the parent plant is prone to decay, developing 'hard' or 'soft rot'. Opinions vary as to the best way to treat these wounds. Some use a mixture of Botrilex (a fungicidal dust) and crushed charcoal with good results, while others paint with methylated spirits, which sterilizes and dries the wound.

One method of producing more offsets, mentioned earlier, is to cut off the main

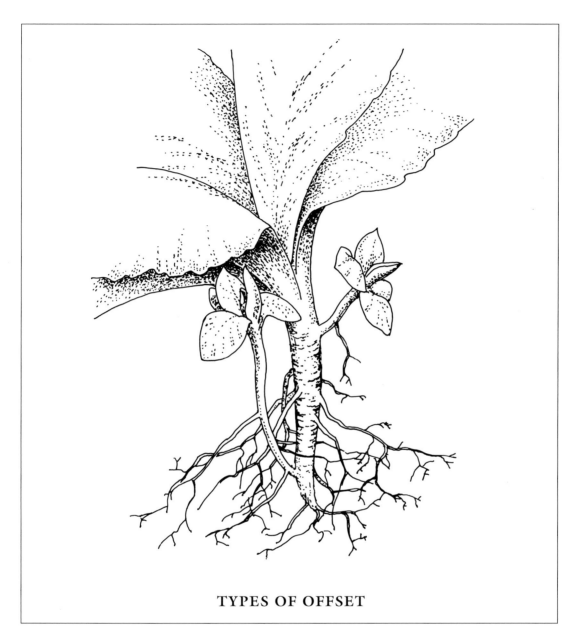

TYPES OF OFFSET

crown just above soil level, preferably immediately after flowering, which is known as topping. This removes the effect of a plant hormone called auxin, produced in plants by the
end shoot, which inhibits the growth of side
shoots. Consequently a large number of offsets can be produced, analogous to 'pinching

back' in other plants to allow them to bush
out. The offsets are allowed to grow on until
early March the following year, when they are
potted on separately, and most flower in
another twelve months. The remaining stump
of the plant can be used as an unrooted cutting or discarded. Peter Ward, who uses this

method extensively, always discards the old tops. This method can be used to cut down on the labour of repotting and results in a large number of young vigorous plants. Another advantage is that offsets have ample light and are not partially or completely hidden by plant leaves and so do not become drawn.

Earlier we mentioned micropropagation or tissue culture that is now used extensively to produce a wide range of plants in huge quantities. In an earlier chapter the saga of 'Tinkerbell' was described and its revival, due to tissue culture by Dr Roger Westcott of the Botany department at the University of Birmingham. Micropropagation involves the production of plants from very small plant parts, tissues, or cells grown aseptically in a test tube or other container, with a rigidly controlled sterile environment and nutritional programme. This is commonly known as tissue culture and was used as a research tool in scientific laboratories for many decades before being applied to the commercial propagation of plants.

The most advanced method is known as meristem culture and has the advantage of being able to produce virus-free plants. Meristems are the growth points of the plant and even in affected plants are often free of virus. Embryo flower-bud material can be used to produce similar virus-free material. The effect is to rejuvenate plants that have been slowly deteriorating due to increasing levels of virus infection. One or two companies specializing in the technique were given, or obtained, many named auriculas with the intention of mass-producing them. The plants were sold to commercial nurseries as very small plantlets to be grown on to flowering size. For some reason this has not worked out as anticipated so that the number of available plants is limited.

More recently Dr F. Taylor of Wye College,

Ashford, Kent has initiated a programme of experimental work by students on tissue culture of auricula leaves as well as a study of viruses affecting the plants.

While interesting and commercially important, meristem or tissue culture is an expensive and complicated laboratory procedure and is not something within the scope of many amateurs. However, in the USA 'do-it-yourself' kits are available but not, to our knowledge, in the UK.

Plants purchased from tissue-cultured stock tend to have excess amounts of growth hormone in their system and may produce forests of offsets for years afterwards. An example is 'Lovebird' where tissue-cultured plants will offset and offset without ever flowering. Some varieties offset only slowly, 'Largo' being an example, failing to develop under tissue culture.

Peter Ward received plants from the original experiments by Dr Roger Westcott and they all grew well and in character. We can only wonder if the mixed results obtained by commercial laboratories are due to a lack of understanding of auriculas; or too much emphasis on the desire to produce them in huge quantities. Some specialist auricula nurserymen routinely have relatively small numbers, about 500, produced by this method.

AURICULA GROWERS' YEAR

Spring Care

Recent winters have been very mild in the UK and the plants have had little rest, with hardly any check to growth. Even so it is our experience in the south and Midlands that new growth can begin as early as late January, although normally it is a little later. The dull green look of the fat central bud assumes a lighter, brighter hue and the plants begin to unfold their leaves. At first the process is very slow but then accelerates. Once this is obvious watering should begin, ideally by standing the clay pots in 2–3 in (5–8 cm) of water for a few minutes, while those in plastics can be given a light watering. Do not overdo it, just sufficient to encourage new growth. As growth increases so can watering, and from February to May it should be generous to copious. If the plants are allowed to dry out during this period flowering may be affected.

By early March flower stems are rising fast and some plants may even be in bloom, often show selfs but also the occasional edged plant and Alpine variety. The peak flowering period of the show selfs is normally the beginning of April and many find that they are over before the date of the main flower shows. This will vary in different parts of the country. Because of this factor many fine selfs never see the show bench. This is compounded by the thin petalled flowers lasting only a few days.

Edged plants, doubles and Alpines are another matter. Most will flower during the period of the main shows, i.e. late April and early May. Many green-edged plants flower at or around showtime and, with the pips remaining in good condition for at least ten days, are easier to manage. Doubles and Alpines are both quite long-lasting flowers.

Last to bloom are the greys and whites: some do not flower until mid-May. On the other hand odd plants will sometimes flower much earlier, just to confuse matters. Treatment of plants during this time consists of keeping them well watered and, at the beginning of March, a liquid feed can be given at half strength; repeat this two weeks later. Some growers advocate a nitrogen feed, especially for doubles and Alpines, to give the plants a good start. Others think a high potash fertilizer like Phostrogen or Chempak No. 8 is all that is needed. Diluted tomato fertilizers are also suitable as they have a high potash content. Another alternative is to carefully push Phostrogen tablets (NPK 8–11–23), one per pot, into the compost. All auriculas respond to sensible feeding but this should not be overdone.

New fertilizers incorporating growth hormones have been coming on to the market recently. It is possible that such products may encourage better flowering in auriculas. Nothing is certain but they are worth trying.

An important habit is to handle your plants frequently and this is crucial during the flowering period. It should become second nature throughout most of the year. By doing this any problem that arises can quickly be identified and remedial action taken.

We referred earlier to the problem of clay pots becoming dirty and slimy, making them unpleasant to handle. It is imperative that cleaning is undertaken early in the year before the plants are well advanced, or problems may result.

Throughout the winter months the plants have been bunched together, the pots as close as possible to provide some measure of insulation. As growth begins the amount of space needed by each plant increases rapidly and must be catered for. The main problem concerns those plants that have mealed foliage. It is easy to smear the meal and spoil the look of the plant. Make sure they are adequately spaced and do not encroach on their neighbours. You must also be careful not to splash water on the leaves creating the same effect. Handling plants needs care and attention.

One other essential task remains and that is shading of the greenhouse. Auriculas don't like hot sun and, in the south, may need some protection from early March. As the sun warms up increase the shading to as many as three layers of mesh. Maximum ventilation must be given to create the cool shady conditions that the plants prefer. It is our belief that adequate shading is a very important element in the successful growing of auriculas and often insufficient attention is paid to it.

Certain other things need to be done now, but as they concern the final appearance of the plant they will be discussed under Exhibiting.

Summer Care

When the plants have flowered, and the shows are over, some growers will remove the flower heads, although not from plants that are being used for hybridizing. Others who grow them purely for pleasure will allow them to wither naturally, removing unwanted seed heads to save the plant's energy. The flower stem should be allowed to wither and turn yellow: it should not be removed when green as this may leave a wound, allowing the entry of fungus spores. When yellow and dry it can be plucked out without difficulty.

It is during June, July and August that the plants are most at risk. After the vigorous spring growth, when the plant leaves reach their maximum size, and particularly if it is warm, auriculas seem to enter a torpid phase. They do little other than sit on the bench looking unhappy. Watering enters a crucial stage and must be done with considerable care: gradually reduce it and keep the compost just moist. The plants must be well shaded and as cool as possible. A mist spray should be given in the evening of hot days and close watch kept for pest attack. Remove yellowed leaves that, if ready, will come away with a gentle tug. Check the plants in the morning by testing the leaves. Just flick the leaf with your finger to see if it needs water. When all is well the leaves will feel crisp and springy. If the compost is moist and the leaves limp you have problems; use a moisture meter if in doubt. During the day even well-shaded

plants will go limp in very hot weather so don't be fooled into thinking they need water — if in doubt do not water. Auriculas store a certain amount of water in the carrot and leaves and will stand being dry for several days or longer. During some holidays they have been left, by both authors, for up to two weeks on damp sand/grit, after a thorough initial watering, and suffered little. It is better of course to have someone water the plants for you providing they are competent to do so.

The ideal place for auriculas in high summer is a north-facing frame where the plants are not exposed to sun. Plunging clay pots in sand, as practised by growers of Alpines, maintains an even temperature and reduces watering. If you are able to put the plants in a cool shady spot, and they are safe against other dangers, it is advisable to do so.

If trouble arises the various signs of rot can be identified as follows: in the early morning, if the crown of the plant is firm but the outer leaves remain lax then root rot may be the cause, assuming the pot is not dry; if the surface of the pot remains moist and moss begins to grow suspect root rot; if the crown inclines to one side or an offset becomes limp you have root rot.

Crown rot may also appear and if the centre fails to grow but offsets come up all around this is a sure sign. A yellowing at the base of the leaves, with the plant assuming a sickly appearance, also indicates crown rot. Finally, growth resumes at the end of August and any plant that looks unhappy at this time may have root rot. Crown rot normally means the loss of the plant but you can often save offsets which tend to proliferate when this condition occurs. Plants with root rot can usually be saved providing it is identified sufficiently early. Remove all dead and dying roots and brown spots in the carrot, cauterize any wounds on the carrot and repot in a more open mix with plenty of sharp grit/sand. When watering such invalids add a suitable fungicide like Benlate to the water. Often plants will recover but regular renewal of plants, especially by the 'topping' method, and an open compost will prevent rot from becoming a problem.

To sum up, the summer months are the most dangerous time for the auricula; plants must be kept as cool and well shaded as possible and carefully watered. The auricula hates hot dry conditions and if they are combined with careless watering heavy losses will occur, especially of the show auricula group.

Autumn Care

When repotting and potting on have been completed, ideally by early September, the plants will begin to settle into their new compost and make new growth. This is not as vigorous as that of the late-spring period, when the leaves reach maximum size. Nevertheless it is an important time and may determine the flowering performance the following spring. When this secondary growth commences water should be given as necessary but again don't overdo it.

It has often been said that the embryo trusses form in the heart of the plant during early autumn. During attempts to tissue culture the first auriculas, embryo trusses were discovered in July when the plants were dissected. This suggested the truss started much earlier than had been believed and may explain why very hot dry summers are followed by poor flowering. Nevertheless, the assumption is that the autumn is the key time and a little judicious feeding may help the process. With late repotting the compost is still fresh and needs little, if any, supplementing. A foliar feed can help the plants though and PBI Fillip is beneficial. Maxicrop is popular with some

growers both as a foliar feed and added to the watering can. In the absence of autumn frosts Chempak 0–10–10 can be used to firm and mature the growth. This contains no nitrogen and can also be used to combat lush growth of any sort. Take care when watering not to lodge any water in the heart of the plant, because of the risk of crown rot, and remove yellowing leaves.

One phenomenon that has caused much soul-searching amongst auricula enthusiasts is that of 'autumn trusses'. In some years many plants will put up flowering stems in late autumn. There are two schools of thought about this, one believing it causes no harm and a lack of them bodes ill the following spring; the other that the appearance of an autumn truss will prevent the plant from flowering well in the spring. This argument has raged for many years but has not been decided either way.

Plants that have spent the summer in frames may be left there until the end of September but should then be returned to the greenhouse. All shading should be removed by early September and the glass given a good clean.

Winter Care

Once the first real frosts arrive the plants assume winter garb, a dismal looking appearance. The outer leaves die off and the foliage is much reduced, sometimes in severe weather to a fat central bud. In many recent winters plants have remained quite leafy due to the mild temperatures. During this time little is required other than removing dead leaves before they develop botrytis, and making sure no water lodges in the crown of the plant. It is better to leave the leaves until they are brown and shrivelled, providing no sign of botrytis develops, in which case they must be removed at once. Watch out for drips from the greenhouse ventilators or other places. If this happens the whole plant can rot away surprisingly quickly. Watering must be very carefully administered but the plants should not be allowed to dry out completely.

The best method of watering for clay pots is to stand them in a few inches of water for a minute or so. During frosty weather the leaves go limp and it is not easy to tell whether plants need water or not. If they are subjected to persistent frost while dust-dry the leaves remain limp and may never recover. Fred Buckley determined whether plants needed water in winter by testing the tip of the central bud; if slightly soft then water was needed. Do not water at all when temperatures are below freezing as it will only turn to ice.

Should the plants be given any form of winter protection? Apart from the necessary overhead cover against rain we suspect the answer is no. Auriculas are bone hardy and providing they have not been grown 'soft' will stand cold and freezing weather without any trouble. They may look miserable but then many plants do at this time of year. It has often been said that the final flowering can be adversely affected if the immature buds are exposed to late spells of frost. This is suspected to be one cause of deformed florets and generally poor flower trusses. Not everyone is convinced and some have carried out experiments to try to prove or disprove the theory without conclusive results. A number of people do keep their greenhouses 'frost free' with sufficient heat to prevent the temperature from going below freezing, especially in March and April. This tends to bring the plants on a little earlier and is also more comfortable for the grower when tending the plants. As for plunging plants during winter it is well known that camellias, rhododendrons, and double primroses, to name a few can die during very severe weather when the roots are frozen in pots, but survive in the open ground. While auriculas in pots are not killed by extreme cold, except perhaps if they are kept too wet, they would probably benefit from winter plunging providing the plunge material is dry.

Finally, one must keep a close eye for the beginning of new growth which generally occurs in late January or early February, when the yearly cycle begins again.

7 Raising new varieties

One of the most interesting aspects of growing auriculas is the challenge of raising new hybrids; indeed many keen growers would say that this is the most fascinating aspect of all. It has always been of prime importance since the supply of good quality plants, especially in the show category, is insufficient to meet demand. In addition all varieties deteriorate after a number of years and it is essential that new plants are introduced to replace them.

Auricula breeding began in the sixteenth century, initially by collecting seed from the better varieties, with no real system or plan, as the sexuality of plants was not then known. The number of seedlings raised must have been enormous and it has often been said that the 'old growers' were pleased if they obtained one good seedling out of a thousand.

Early in the nineteenth century plant breeders, influenced by experiments in controlled pollination by J. G. Koelreuter, began to select both parents for hybridizing. The early auricula growers like Emmerton and Hogg did this by isolating the plants and hoping the bees would do the rest. Crossing like with like was also introduced and later hand fertilization, which gave a greater degree of control.

F. R. McQuown in his well-known book *Plant Breeding for Gardeners*, published in 1963, stated that the majority of successful breeders fall into three classes. Those who assert that genetics is no good at all, those who say it seems very interesting but personally do not understand it, and those who sprinkle their writings and conversation with numerous genetical terms that they do not understand. The problem for the amateur is that the number of plants he has room to raise is generally insufficient to permit the proper application of scientific principles. To quote F. R. McQuown:

> The keen grower who observes his plants closely will gradually build up a subconscious store of knowledge of minute details of his plants. After a time he will suddenly get ideas of crossing certain plants together without knowing consciously why he does so, and very often these lead to startling successes.

This is certainly the case with auricula hybridizers. Some of the most successful do so by following their intuition or hunches but we would not suggest that basic scientific principles be ignored completely as an understanding of them may certainly help.

With auriculas, particularly edged varieties, the requirements are so numerous that the problem is especially complicated. In addition many of the most desirable features, such as a smooth paste, are recessive and tend to disappear. In the Alpine section less characters are looked for and a higher success rate is possible.

With double auriculas, as with all double flowers, the problem is rather different. In

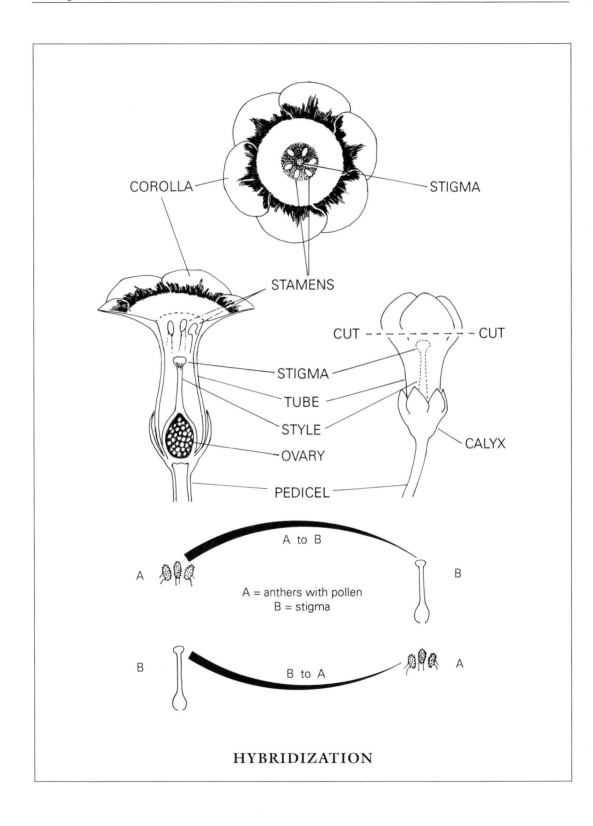

COROLLA

STIGMA

STAMENS

CUT - - - - - CUT

STIGMA

TUBE

STYLE

OVARY

CALYX

PEDICEL

A to B

A   B

A = anthers with pollen
B = stigma

B

B to A   A

HYBRIDIZATION

nature all flowers are single, with male and female parts for the production of seed to perpetuate the species. Double flowers do sometimes occur in nature but invariably die out and it is only through vegetative propagation, or the modern technique of tissue culture, that they can be maintained

Border auriculas are less complicated as they are grown for effect and are not subject to the stringent requirements of the other sorts. Nevertheless the introduction of brighter, clearer colours on robust plants is a desirable aim.

Most auricula hybridizers would say that the best policy is to cross the best plants available, of similar type, and hope for the best!

POLLINATION

The hand-pollination of auricula flowers is a simple process and consists of transferring pollen from the selected pollinator to the stigma (i.e. the upper part of the pistil) of the seed parent. The pistil is the entire female organ of the flower and includes the stigma, style and ovary. With double auriculas it is slightly more complicated but unlike double primroses pollen can usually be found.

Border auriculas can be either pin- or thrum-eyed and many of the named varieties are pin-eyed. The natural method is to pollinate a pin-eyed plant from a thrum and this is very easy to achieve.

In show and Alpine auriculas pin-eyed plants are not acceptable and the leading growers would all cross thrum x thrum. The only exception might be if a seedling appeared that was otherwise excellent apart from being pin-eyed. This makes the process of crossing a little more complicated as it is more difficult to transfer pollen from thrum to thrum. While pin-eyed plants do still turn up in most seedling crosses the continuous

breeding of thrums has now reduced this to a low percentage in show auriculas.

The flower of the seed parent is carefully cut back using a sharp pair of small nail scissors so that the stigma is exposed, or alternatively the petals are carefully torn outwards with the fingers. Take care not to damage the stigma when doing this – it is easily done. The stigma, when receptive, exudes a sticky fluid so that the pollen grains will stick to it; it is most receptive when the flowers are half open or in the 'big bud' stage, as it is called. If the flowers are not sufficiently open the stigma may not be receptive. Conversely, if the flowers are too mature or 'old' failure is also probable. The potency of pollen remains for a considerable time if it is stored in cool dry conditions. In the auricula the male parts, or stamens, are attached to the inside of the petals and when ripe burst and shed pollen. This can be checked by examining them under a glass; if ready they have a fluffy appearance.

There are several ways of transferring pollen of which the time-honoured method of using a fine camel-hair brush is one. When this is done the brush must be cleaned and sterilized by dipping in methylated spirit and dried, after every pollination, which is time-consuming. One of the most common methods used by the majority of auricula breeders is to use fine-pointed tweezers to transfer pollen, by picking off a ripe stamen and gently touching it to the stigma. Pollen can also be transferred straight from the flower. With this latter method the flower is removed; the petals are torn open, then folded down and outwards so that the stamens stand proud. Held between finger and thumb the stamens are brushed gently against the stigma and shaken slightly. In all three of these methods the process may be repeated several times to ensure a good covering of pollen. Usually two to three pips are pollinated on each plant, all other flowers being removed. When finished the stigma is examined under a powerful magnifying glass to check that pollen is adhering to it. If successful the green stigma will have a yellow tinge and the individual grains of pollen can be seen.

David Hadfield pollinates several pips on the plants he uses as seed parents. He feels that as the parent plant will be of no use for exhibition in the following year this is quite acceptable and likely to produce more seed. As seed is rarely abundant, especially with edged show auriculas, this is well worth trying. When completed a second plant label is put in the pot with the cross and date clearly written on it in indelible ink or horticultural pencil. Some growers like to mark the seed heads by tying coloured wool around the footstalk to prevent removal when routinely removing dead flower stems. The plant is then watered and put in a safe position in the greenhouse or frame for the seed to ripen; this takes approximately two to three months depending on the weather. Seed bearing takes a lot of energy from the parent plant and it must be well watered and given an occasional liquid feed.

Some advocate covering the plants in various ways to prevent accidental cross-pollination by bees or other insects but most growers do not do this. Once the petals are removed so is the attraction of nectar and scent, and bees are no longer interested.

If the cross has taken, the footstalk and ovary remain green; a premature browning and shrivelling of the footstalk indicates failure. When the seed is ripe the stalk turns brown, followed by the plump seedpod which should begin to open. Auricula seed is usually ripe before the pod starts to split and providing the capsule is brown it is quite in order to remove it and carefully crack it open. This does have its dangers and the cautious grower will wait until a slight split appears before removing the capsule. It can then be put in a clean saucer or other receptacle until the pod dries out and opens fully, depositing the seed on to the saucer.

In the past it has been said that fertilization is more likely to be effective carried out in the early morning. This is not supported by any evidence and hybridizers generally will successfully carry out the process at their convenience during different times of the day.

SOWING THE SEED

Once the seed is harvested you are faced with two choices: either to sow immediately or keep it until the following spring. A consensus is beginning to emerge among growers in favour of sowing the seed at once. If this is done germination is often very rapid, literally within days. In addition the seedlings grow quickly and may in favourable years be pricked out by late autumn. This has the added advantage that they may flower a year earlier. In any event auricula seedlings are very hardy and overwinter without qualms. Some years ago a Scottish grower, writing in the Northern yearbook, reported that seedlings in his greenhouse had been submerged under water due to a broken pane in the roof. This soon turned to ice and the tiny plants were encased in a solid block. After several weeks the ice thawed and the seedlings 'shook themselves' and continued growing as if nothing had happened. We are not suggesting such a harsh regime is ideal but it does show how tough auricula seedlings can be.

The alternative is to keep the seed until the following year, sowing it in late February. Various receptacles can be used to store the seed including paper packets, small seed envelopes or the transparent plastic containers that hold rolls of 35 mm film. Plastic bags should not be used as mould can develop. They should be put in a screw-top jar (an old 2-litre ice cream carton is also ideal), and placed in the fridge. Note the lid should be firmly on the container and it must be in the fridge not the freezer compartment. The salad box is ideal and so are the trays in the door.

Whether one sows in autumn or spring the procedure is the same. First choose a container in which to sow the seed. The type of container is a matter of choice and will depend to some extent on the number of seeds. If few, a small 2½ in (6.35 cm) or 3 in (7.62 cm) plastic pot may be all that is needed. Garden centres sell excellent plastic seed trays of various sizes. Some growers use old margarine or butter tubs, while even plastic microwave dishes are utilized by one famous hybridizer. All these *ad hoc* containers must have holes drilled in the base so that surplus moisture drains away.

The compost is also a matter of personal choice and considerable and surprising variation exists amongst growers. David Hadfield uses his normal potting mix with added sand; Allan Hawkes John Innes No 2 without modification. Gwen Baker favours an equal mix of J.I. No. 1 and grit while Martin Sheader uses fifty per cent J.I. No. 1 plus fifty per cent Universal compost with a little fine grit. Derek Telford, Peter Ward and Arthur Delbridge all favour a peat or peat-based soilless compost.

There are numerous good seed composts, either peat or peat-based, that give excellent results. Fisons Levington Compost, Baby Bio and Arthur Bowers are all reliable, providing they are fresh.

The procedure for sowing seed, noting that all primula seeds need light to germinate, is as follows:

1. Fill the container with compost and level it by tapping or gently pressing using a suitable flat object.
2. Place in a tray of clean water and allow the compost to soak this up by capillary action until the surface is moist.
3. Remove and allow to drain for thirty minutes or longer.
4. Sprinkle the seed evenly over the compost.
5. Cover with a thin layer of coarse grit or vermiculite.
6. Place in a large tray with a plastic cover or use a sheet of glass, clingfilm or plastic bag to cover.
7. Place in a cool position with plenty of light.
8. Inspect regularly until germination takes place.
9. Remove the plastic cover.

When using soilless compost stand the tray in only one or two inches of water at most. If the compost is on the dry side, not unusual, it may be displaced and forced up out of the tray.

To ensure even distribution some growers mix a little fine sand with the seed.

Sometimes if germination is delayed and conditions are very moist, mould or a green scum may appear on the surface of the tray. Spraying with Phostrogen Safer Garden Fungicide will keep this in check. The plastic cover should be removed only after the main germination has taken place; often one or two seedlings will appear prematurely.

Some soilless composts, composed solely of peat, can cause problems when you attempt to prick out the seedlings. The roots become entangled in the peat and it is easy to tear them off. One way of preventing this is to add perlite, well mixed in; the resulting mixture falls away from the roots more easily.

When the seedlings are large enough to handle, usually when they have three or four leaves, they should be pricked out into a standard-sized seed tray, 8 in (20.32 cm) x 14 in (35.56 cm), about 1 in ($^1/_2$ cm) apart. They are then moved once more several weeks later into a large 12 in (30.48 cm) x 23 in (58.42 cm) tray, some 3 in (7.62 cm) inches apart – approximately thirty-six to the tray, where they remain until they flower some eighteen months to two years after initial germination. Of course various other types of containers may be used instead of plastic trays but they are probably the most convenient.

The above procedures are the same for all auriculas but when crossed the different types do not behave in a similar fashion.

SHOW AURICULAS

The shows, divided into edged and selfs including stripes, are the most difficult. Edged plants in particular may only produce small amounts of seed. Often the seedpod, although fat and healthy looking, will be empty, the embryo seeds shrivelled to tiny black specks. Occasionally a bumper crop of seed is produced and when this happens the chances of success are greater. The renowned 'old growers' were reputed to be pleased if one good seedling emerged from a thousand. Fortunately, crossing modern varieties brings a better percentage than this but it is still very low compared with many other plants.

The theoretical procedure when crossing is to select two suitable plants possessing a combination of desirable features. They are then crossed both ways and it is hoped the good features will combine in some of the progeny. It would be desirable to get a slightly wider body colour here, a rounder tube there, perhaps a smoother paste. In reality this rarely happens with edged plants and the resulting seedlings will be a very mixed bag. There are usually a number of frilly-petalled dark selfs

and a few muddy colours. The edged seedlings contain all sorts of variations, mostly ugly, bearing little resemblance to the parents. Fancy auriculas appear as well as body colours other than black, even though both parents had a black body colour. If you know your parent plants, and have a little or perhaps large slice of luck, something good may appear. This may seem disconcerting to those wishing to try their luck at hybridizing. Do not despair as crosses between many modern varieties do produce rather better results, although the percentage of really good plants is still very low.

Earlier crossing both ways was referred to as the orthodox method. In reality not all hybridizers do this and several cross one way only. This has come about, we believe, due to the low success rate with auricula seedlings. Certain plants have been found, or were thought, to be superior as seed parents and others as pollinators. Consequently efforts have been concentrated on them to try and improve the success rate. Such plants are called 'pre-potent' and examples are 'Teem', 'Melody' and 'HMR1' as pollinators, with 'Walhampton' and 'Fleminghouse' as seed parents. Raisers used jealously to keep such information to themselves but modern growers are more open and share such findings freely.

Selfs are far more reliable than edged plants, set more seed and a better percentage of good plants can be expected. Crossing the best yellow selfs produces some excellent plants of which a few should be up to show standard. The reds seem a little more difficult and have not improved in recent years as much as anticipated. Achieving good form and brighter colours has not proved easy with seedlings deficient in one or the other, rarely combining both. Blue selfs are the odd man out and will produce large quantities of seed but despite this good ones remain rare. Some good dark selfs have been raised and considerable effort is going into raising other colours.

Stripes are a recent development and have special problems of their own. It has taken many years to reach the present position and there is still room for considerable improvement. Form leaves a great deal to be desired and the search for new colour combinations goes on. Their devotees maintain that the latest varieties are approaching edged standards in respect of tube, paste and roundness of petal. Others would maintain that this is somewhat optimistic and further progress is necessary.

Once the seedlings have flowered the best are selected for growing on. The thing to look for is quality and this not as simple as it might seem. Edged plants vary enormously and may not settle down for several years. Many seedlings, whether edged or selfs, will produce a beautiful maiden truss which is never repeated; physical deterioration sets in and the plant fades away. This aspect of the behaviour of new seedlings is the one that tends to be voiced. On the other hand the reverse may happen and after a few years an improvement takes place, the plant becoming more stable. It is not suggested that 'geese' turn into 'swans'; seedlings must show some good qualities to be retained in the first instance. The lesson of all this is to have patience and persevere with promising seedlings as long as possible. Self discipline, in selecting only the best, and judgment in persisting with them are also important.

ALPINE AURICULAS

With Alpine auriculas things are considerably simpler as fewer characteristics of excellence are looked for. To begin with only two basic types, gold and light centres, have to be considered. Within each type considerable colour variation occurs ranging from brown, maroon and crimson shades in the gold centres to pink, violet and purple shades in the light centres. Variations in colouring, 'Sirius' being the most extreme example, and sharper graduations in the colour shading have appeared in recent years. Not all raisers like these new developments but they do have their advocates.

The difficulties experienced with shows, particularly edged plants, in setting seed are not such a problem with the Alpines.

Once again the 'illegal' cross of thrum x thrum is the norm since, as with shows, pin-eyed plants are not acceptable to auricula growers, other than in garden or border auriculas.

The leading modern hybridizer of Alpine auriculas, Derek Telford, says that he still finds too many pin-eyed plants amongst his seedlings that are otherwise beautiful flowers. He will not use pin-eyed plants for breeding because of this. Derek also rejects plants for breeding purposes that have the stigma within the stamens rather than below. Another phenomenom that occurs is the 'half-way house' between the thrums and pins, where the stigma is neither above nor below the stamens – referred to as a 'mid-pin' flower. Such plants are not necessarily disqualified on the show bench but one can see the dangers if used for hybridizing.

Although concentrating in recent years on striped auriculas Allan Hawkes is also well known for his hybridizing of Alpines. Allan continued the work of C. F. Hill, known as 'Fred' to his friends, who raised a series of gold-centred seedlings between 1957 and the late 1960s. Fred by this time was very elderly and wished to pass on his knowledge and 'strain' to someone who would continue his work. Allan agreed to do so, was sworn to secrecy and in due course received the information along with plants and seed.

Fred was convinced of the prepotency of a Haysom gold centre called 'Bratley' which he used as his original seed parent. His method was to cross the progeny of each generation back to the original parents, quite often in turn. As Allan pointed out Jack Ballard was similarly motivated, with a plant called 'Mrs G. Savory'. The famous Northern grower Frank Faulkner also started his hybridizing career by concentrating his efforts on a plant called 'Tom Jones', crossing it to 'Irene', 'Albert Mottershead', 'Dr Pegge', 'Verdi' and others. 'Tom Jones' had a bright centre but was faulty in that it had a 'mid-pin'.

'Bratley', described by Haysom as being a 'rich crimson', was actually more of a brownish shade and had a tendency to pass this on to its offspring. The 'Hill' alpines were so identified by this brown-orange shade that it became known to many as 'Hill colour'. Later the brightly coloured 'Forge', raised by Frank Faulkner, was introduced to try and brighten up the strain which it did in varieties like 'Bolero' and 'Janie Hill'. The family tree supplied to Allan, never previously revealed, was as follows:

1957 'Bratley' x 'Mrs E. Goodman'
　　　(= 'Tally-Ho')
1959 'Bratley' x 'Tally-Ho' (= 'Janie Hill')
1961 'Janie Hill' x 'Tally-Ho' (= 'Fresco'
　　　and 'Kelso')
1960 'Mrs E. Goodman' x 'Verdi'
　　　(= 'Rodeo')
1962 'Tally-Ho' x 'Rodeo' (= 'Shako')
1964 'Bratley' x 'Shako' (= 'Bolero' and
　　　'Cameo')
1965 'Shako' x 'Verdi' (= 'Dado')
1965 'Rodeo' x 'Verdi' (= 'Halo')
1965 'Shako' x 'Forge' (= 'Bilbao')
1966 'Bratley' x 'Shako', 'Bratley' x 'Fresco',
　　　'Bratley' x 'Bolero', 'Shako' x 'Bolero'.

This is a good example of what is referred to as 'line-breeding'.

Other snippets from Fred's letters, passed on by Allan, are that 'Mrs E. Goodman' came from a cross between 'Downton' x 'Bratley', 'Forge' x 'Golda Goodman' produced 'Domino', 'Angelo' and 'Akimbo' while 'Angelo' x 'Forge' gave 'Flamingo'.

Allan felt that the possibilities had been almost exhausted with the plants used by Fred and crossed his seedlings with some of the more brightly coloured gold centres like 'Blossom'. Allan is still crossing Alpines and has encountered an interesting phenomenon where the 'custard centre' 'Sirius' is involved. Usually he crosses one way only but has found that some plants, with a 'Sirius' parent on each side, can be deficient in pollen, the anthers don't open, or have a strange looking stigma.

Many other raisers have produced excellent seedlings and there is no doubt that crossing the better varieties gives a very good chance of success. As a result the numbers of new seedlings, both light and gold centres, being introduced in recent years are increasing.

DOUBLE AURICULAS

Crossing double auriculas is slightly different. As explained in the chapter on doubles the genes that control doubling are recessive. If a single plant is known to have a double parent it will still carry the necessary genes in a hidden form in the F1 generation. Such plants are useful in producing doubles when crossed, preferably with a double rather than another F1 single. Gwen Baker has recently attempted to introduce pure-red doubles by using the red self show auricula 'Pat' as a pollen parent crossed with an unnamed red seedling. The resulting seedlings will probably all be single and it is hoped that by cross-

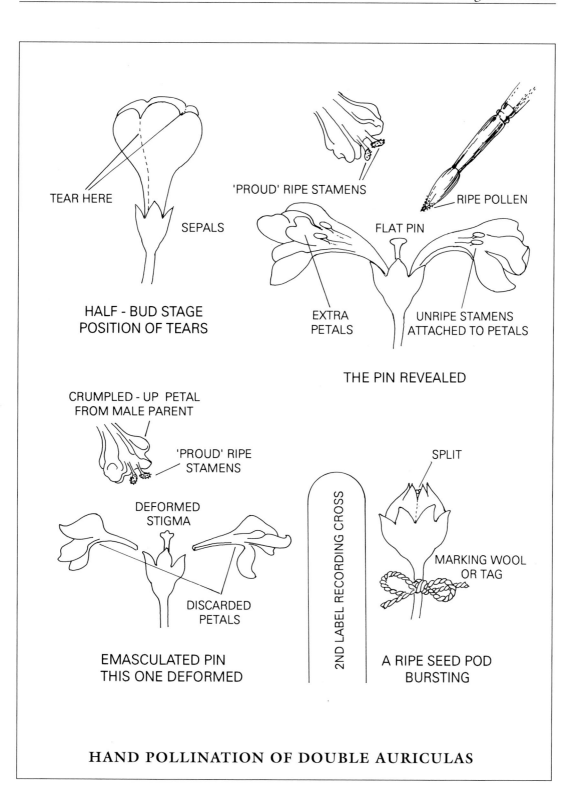

TEAR HERE

SEPALS

HALF - BUD STAGE
POSITION OF TEARS

'PROUD' RIPE STAMENS

RIPE POLLEN

FLAT PIN

EXTRA
PETALS

UNRIPE STAMENS
ATTACHED TO PETALS

THE PIN REVEALED

CRUMPLED - UP PETAL
FROM MALE PARENT

'PROUD' RIPE
STAMENS

DEFORMED
STIGMA

DISCARDED
PETALS

EMASCULATED PIN
THIS ONE DEFORMED

2ND LABEL RECORDING CROSS

SPLIT

MARKING WOOL
OR TAG

A RIPE SEED POD
BURSTING

HAND POLLINATION OF DOUBLE AURICULAS

ing two together, to produce an F2 generation, the desired bright-red seedling double may result. The other proviso is that many doubles, on inspection, will prove to have a deformed stigma and be incapable of bearing seed. However, such a plant may have a perfect stigma on one of the last pips to open on the truss. An example is the red double 'Doyen' raised by Gwen Baker where this has occurred on at least one occasion. Although doubling is recessive, all present doubles must have had the single genes eliminated and bear at least two sets of chromosomes carrying the doubling genes. The theory is that the selected doubles, one of which has a functional stigma and can bear seed, are now crossed together. If successful, amongst the seedlings will be one which has the desired form and doubling and is an attractive colour. This is the theory; in practice you take a chance and hope for the best!

Recently Mr Ken Whorton sent one of us details of the parentage of his new winning seedlings. They are included here to show that in almost every case the parent plants, in one case the grandparents and great grandparents, were existing doubles.

'Lima' A lime-yellow double that came from a 'Hoghton Gem' x 'Mary' cross. Mary has a perfect stigma and bears seed regularly.

'Calypso' A soft, orange-marmalade colour from Unnamed pink double x 'Westcott Pride' x 'Hoghton Gem'.

'May Morning' Salmon-pink suffused yellow from the same cross and seedpod as 'Calypso'. Three existing doubles were in the parentage.

'Digit' Gold from 'Bilton' x 'Mary' x 'Westcott Pride' x 'Hoghton Gem'

In the final case 'Bilton' is an older yellow show self, so the F1 generation would most certainly have been single. The resultant

seedling was crossed with 'Westcott Pride', a red double, producing an F2 generation, and crossed for a third generation to 'Hoghton Gem'. This latter plant appears to be pre-potent as it features in all these crosses. Crossing the F2 generation together, or using the same plant continuously is another example of line breeding.

Dr Martin Sheader began hybridizing doubles with plants raised from Barnhaven seed. He has continued this line, rarely introducing plants from other raisers. Martin is producing some wonderful doubles and the colour range is widening year by year. Some lines followed have not yet been successful, for example attempts to raise bright-red and also blue doubles starting with single show auricula selfs as the seed parents. He has found that heavily mealed plants tend to produce double seedlings with too much meal on the flowers, spoiling the appearance.

Another tip from Martin is to follow through to the F2 generation. 'Diamond' produced poor offspring in the F1 generation but the F2s were much better with some very acceptable plants.

BORDER AURICULAS

Borders are the easiest of auriculas to raise since the named varieties are a mixture of pin- and thrum-eyed plants, with pins in the majority. It is very simple to pollinate a pin-eyed plant from a thrum but you can also cross 'pin x pin', another 'illegal cross'. The petals are torn and folded back, removing the pin as you do so, and pollen transferred to the proposed seed parent. The resulting seedlings grow just as vigorously as a normal 'thrum x pin' cross and seed is produced in similar amounts.

The majority of borders fall into two groups; those resembling show auriculas in some way and those that resemble Alpines. Some plants exist that don't quite fall into either category but they are few and far between.

It would be possible to bring about a large improvement in these plants were someone really to concentrate on them. We need better colours, clearer and brighter to go with the vigour that some plants undoubtedly possess. At the moment, while popular with many enthusiasts, they are the poor relations of the auricula world.

8 Pest & diseases

Auriculas are tough hardy plants that are not troubled by very many pests or fungal diseases. Providing vigilance is maintained, and remedial action taken as soon as problems are noticed, they are not difficult to control, although vine weevil and red spider have caused increasing difficulties in recent years.

PESTS

Greenfly Aphids (various species)

Greenfly make their appearance in early spring. At this time of year a spray cannot be used, if the plants are intended for exhibition, since it will spoil the foliage and flowers of any mealed plant. Usually a systemic insecticide added to the watering can at spray strength will eradicate them. The normal method advocated to control greenfly in greenhouses or frames is fumigation, at regular intervals, with an appropriate smoke or aerosol. Many of the structures used by auricula growers are too open for this to work well, so spraying with a recommended insecticide is more practical but only after flowering is finished. Overall this is a minor pest that does not trouble auriculas, with their tough leaves, in any significant way except that they can introduce virus.

Where the grower is opposed to the use of insecticides he or she will have to rely on brushing off the pests with a soft brush; a tedious process that needs repeating fre-quently. The alternative method is to use a small vacuum cleaner of the sort used for cleaning computer keyboards.

Root Aphid (various species)

This is a pest that has been described in previous works, notably Hecker (1971), as 'the most formidable of the auricula pests since it is not always easy to detect, and more difficult to eradicate than greenfly'; more prevalent and severe in drought conditions. It is true that an infected plant will eventually suffer a serious devitalizing effect but this will only occur if the plant's owner is very neglectful. They are usually seen first round the neck of the plant and those visible can be killed by means of a soft brush, dipped in methylated spirits, which instantly dissolves the wool/wax, following up by watering with the insecticide. The root or woolly aphid, as it is more commonly known, can be found at any time of the year but is at its most active during the early part of the year, when the plants commence growth, and during the secondary growth period in late summer to early autumn. The aphids feed on the sap of the roots producing a white powdery wax making them easy to detect; if unchecked they increase rapidly, stunting growth, although rarely killing the host plant. A badly affected plant with damaged roots may succumb to harmful bacteria and fungus. Another concern is that these insects can spread virus diseases.

Black Vine Weevil *(Otiorhynchus sulcatus)*

The vine weevil has become a serious pest of many garden and pot plants in recent years and attacks primulas, including auriculas, particularly when grown in pots. Several species of weevil will attack auriculas but the vine weevil is the most common. One hears many stories of plant losses due to the depredations of the grubs. Plants grown in peat-based composts are especially likely to be attacked.

The adult beetles are just under $\frac{1}{2}$ in (9–10 mm) long and dull black with small, light-brown patches on their roughened wing cases, giving them a speckled appearance. They have elbowed antennae and cannot fly; they walk very slowly. They are excellent climbers and are often found at considerable heights, even on ceilings in houses. Their eyesight is poor but they locate the host plants by smell. The adults do not attack the roots but cause unsightly damage by eating irregular notches, normally U-shaped, from the margins of the leaves. When this type of damage is seen the grubs are certain to follow!

In the greenhouse the adults may emerge in autumn but are more often found in late March to May. In the garden they are active during the summer months and will attack plants growing in the soil, but with less obvious effect. All adult vine weevils are female (a male has yet to be found), and each one can lay up to 1,000 viable eggs over a period of several months, with the peak in June and July. It is almost impossible to prevent them gaining access to greenhouses where they hide during the day, in some dark place, coming out to feed at night.

The minute eggs, which can survive for three to five years in a dry medium, historically peat, are laid on top of the compost and the grubs burrow into the soil when hatched.

At this early stage they are at their most vulnerable and can be destroyed by drenching the compost with a suitable insecticide. They eat the roots and even a single grub causes considerable damage although it may not kill the plant. When several are at work in a pot the root system can be almost totally destroyed and the plant becomes loose and wilts, a slight tug bringing it out of the pot. In some cases, providing the carrot has not been destroyed, it is possible to re-root the top rather like a cutting.

When fully-grown the grubs are about $\frac{1}{2}$ in (10 mm) long but appear shorter as their bodies are curved. They are plump, creamy white with a pale-brown head and have no legs. They pupate in the soil and some adult features, such as legs, antennae and wing pads can be seen on the pupae. Larval damage occurs mainly in autumn and spring when the grubs are becoming fully grown.

The problem with vine weevil is that the grubs, especially when fully grown, have a considerable tolerance to insecticides. At one time the remedy was to incorporate Aldrin dust in the compost which gave almost complete control. Aldrin is now banned and anyone caught using it faces a very substantial fine. The alternative was HCH dust which is also under threat as it belongs to the same group of chemicals as Aldrin, the chlorinated hydrocarbons. HCH is currently still available but is no longer recommended for mixing in composts.

Of the available pesticides a drench of spray-strength HCH, permethrin or pirimiphos-methyl can be used to water the pots. Providing the compost is thoroughly saturated, which may cause other problems, most grubs should be killed, especially if they are not fully grown.

New chemical controls are being developed

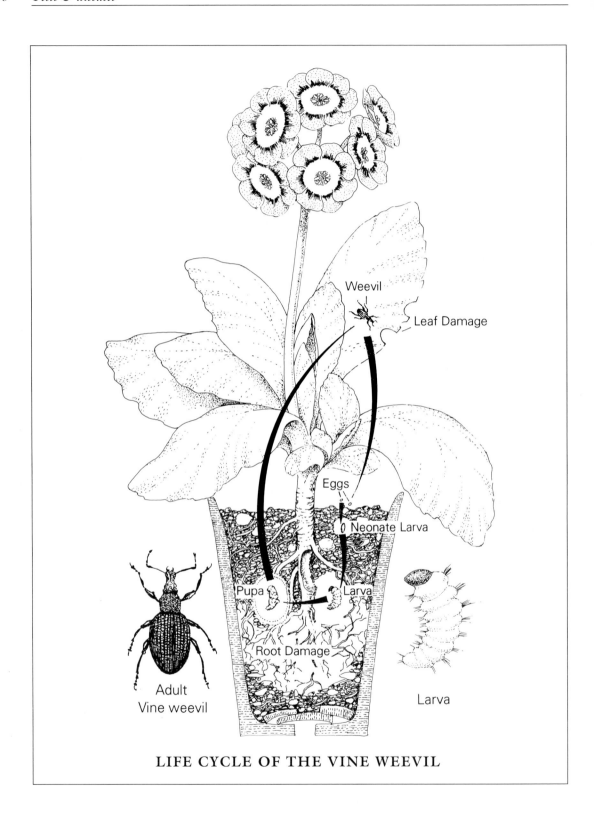

LIFE CYCLE OF THE VINE WEEVIL

but it appears the cost of obtaining pesticide approval for sale to amateurs is so great, well over £1 million has been mentioned, that they may only be available for professional use. One such product recently launched is 'suSCon Green' which is 10 per cent Chlorpyrifos, formulated as a slow-release granule to give two years' or more control over vine weevil in composts. Recently we have heard that attempts are being made to get approval to sell it to amateurs, but this may take a while. Another professional product is 'Cudgel' which is said to be proving effective used as a drench. These products are not for sale to amateurs and it is illegal to use them. Indeed it seems that the range of pesticides available to the amateur grower will continue to decline as concerns grow about their environmental drawbacks.

The latest development, suggested as the only alternative for the amateur grower, is biological control with the nematodes *Heterorhabditis megidis* and *Steinernema bibionis*. They are supplied as millions of nematodes in a concentrated solution, absorbed into a sponge. The microscopic nematodes are squeezed out into water and applied as a drench to pot plants during late summer or when grubs are found to be present. The nematodes are only active between a soil temperature range of 10–21°C (50–70°F) and the compost must not be allowed to dry out. A loose compost, such as peat or peat substitute, is preferred if they are to move freely. The nematodes enter the vine weevil grubs' bodies and release bacteria which cause a fatal infection. The grubs die and the nematodes feed on the bacteria in the decaying bodies. These nematodes also kill sciarid fly larvae as a bonus. The problem is that when the grubs are eliminated the nematodes die and a fresh hatching of weevil eggs may start the process again. Drawbacks appear to be the need for

quite precise temperature and humidity control, something outside the scope of most amateurs, and the grubs also need to be present in some numbers for the nematodes to seek them out.

Amateur packs of nematodes are available for approximately £5–£10 from several sources, one with the trade name of 'Fightagrub' supplied by Fargro Ltd of Littlehampton. The pack can be stored for a short time in a refrigerator but as they are living animals with a short shelf life must be used as soon as possible after receipt. A £5 pack will treat the equivalent of 250 $3\frac{1}{2}$ in (7.62 cm) pots. The development of such biological controls is proceeding rapidly and another product called Biosafe, available from Homebase stores, has just come on the market which can be used for the treatment of vine weevil in pots. In this instance the nematodes are not activated until a special solution is poured into the Biosafe jar. Lukewarm tap water is added to the 'fill' level marked on the jar label, the lid replaced and the contents thoroughly shaken. The solution is poured into a clean watering can and cool water added to make up to two gallons. Once activated you must use it within three hours, although the original pack has a shelf life of two to three months. Biosafe is primarily recommended for outdoor use and will kill several other soil pests in addition to weevils.

Adult weevils can be controlled by spraying or dusting with permethrin, pirimiphos-methyl or HCH applied to the foliage and soil surface at dusk. Keeping your greenhouse in a tidy condition and checking the undersides of pots and trays for hidden weevils – and underneath the staging – will help to reduce numbers. Various other methods of keeping weevils out have been tried or suggested by several inventive growers. The most extreme is to put a moat around the greenhouse, although I'm sure this comment was made tongue in cheek!

Interest in non-toxic methods continues to grow and as weevils cannot fly, preventing them from reaching the plants by erecting physical barriers is a possibility. One suggestion is to use a product called the Trappit Glue Tube. The staging legs of the benches (and elsewhere as necessary) are treated with the tacky substance and the adult weevils get stuck. It should be noted, though, that they will walk across the bodies of weevils, or other debris, that may be trapped in the glue.

Finally, covering the surface of the pots with grit or fine gravel, as practised by growers of alpine plants, also reduces the number of grubs by creating a partial barrier. Dr Martin Sheader did a controlled test on a number of auriculas in pots with and without grit topping. On those pots where grit was used the number of weevil grubs was much reduced although not eliminated.

Fungus Gnats (Sciarid flies)

These small black flies are very common in greenhouses and are attracted by the odour of decaying matter, alighting on any adjacent soil to lay their eggs. The larvae, small whitish translucent maggots with a black head, feed on any rotting vegetable matter they can find.

At one period there was considerable controversy within auricula circles over this minor pest. Several growers who suffered heavy losses through carrot 'rot' were convinced that the sciarid larvae attacking this 'rot' were the cause rather than simply taking advantage of it. The modern use of peat or similar materials as the major constituent of potting composts has brought about something of a population explosion. The result is that the larvae may attack the fine roots of seedlings and cuttings. In severe cases even large plants might be attacked and damaged. Despite this possi-

bility few if any auricula growers report having suffered in this way.

Control of the maggots is by systemic insecticide watered on to the pots. The adults can be controlled by aerosol sprays or by hanging yellow glue traps, available from garden centres, along the benches. They are suspended a few inches above the plants and a variety of flying insects are attracted to them by the colour. The number of insects caught during a season runs into many hundreds and sciarid fly are the most numerous.

Red Spider Mite (Tetranychus urticae)

This is another pest, which together with vine weevil has become a major problem in recent years. The reason is almost certainly the run of hot dry summers we have experienced, providing conditions in which they thrive. In addition the pesticides that are recommended to control red spider do not seem to be very effective and the mites are very difficult to eradicate. Nevertheless, it is worth persevering with sprays, varying the type of insecticide used and paying particular attention to the underside of the leaves. Systemic insecticides work better than contact sprays.

Red spider, which is not a spider at all, is difficult to see with the naked eye but its presence is indicated by a yellow mottling of the leaves. In very bad infestations the leaves turn almost white, then brown as the sap is sucked from them. A plant attacked has an unmistakable appearance which you will soon learn to recognize. The mites cluster on the underside of the leaves which should be examined under a lens for signs of the tiny white webs. Among them the minute yellow mites with dark patches either side of the body will be detected. The mites are less than 1 mm in length but increase rapidly, each new generation appearing approximately every two weeks at 20°C (68°F) and in less than a week at 30°C (86°F). Each adult mite can produce more than 100 eggs over a three-week period and large populations can develop in a short space of time. During the autumn the mites become deep red in colour and leave the plant to hibernate in cracks and crevices. They overwinter without feeding and re-emerge the following spring.

A number of pesticides, 'Malathion' being an example, are quoted as effective against red spider when used as a spray. Quite a number of growers have found that the mites are still alive after such treatment and appear to have developed a resistance to the chemicals. Recently we have been told that Benlate, a fungicide, used at recommended spray strength kills the young mites. The adults are unharmed but treatment at two-weekly intervals will soon eliminate them.

A biological control for red spider is now available: this is the predatory mite *Phytoseiulus persimilis* originating from South America. With a pear-shaped, shiny red body it is slightly larger than the spider mite. Once introduced the predator searches out the mites and will consume many hundreds of them during its life cycle of six to twelve days, depending on temperature. Cost is similar to that for treatment of the vine weevil, £5–10 for a typical amateur-sized greenhouse. Once again temperature is very important as well as timing, as the predator dies once the mites are consumed.

Probably the best way to control red spider is to ensure the conditions in which they thrive do not exist. If you are able to maintain a humid atmosphere in the greenhouse throughout the summer months, by continuous damping down, most growers would maintain the problem does not arise. Those growers who are able to put their plants outside during the summer claim to have no trouble with the pest.

Amongst auriculas the plants with mealed foliage seem to be particularly attractive to red spider and are usually the first to be attacked. This is also difficult to detect and the plants can be in a sorry state before it is realised that the white of the foliage is not simply caused by meal. Primroses or gold-laced polyanthus in the same structure are always preferred by the mites to auriculas and *Primula marginata* is also very prone to attack.

Whitefly *(Trialeurodes vaporariorum)*

This is another pest that has become more of a nuisance in recent summers. It is a small moth-like insect that thrives in an unduly dry atmosphere and again is difficult to control. Eggs are laid on the underside of newly-developed leaves and hatch into small immobile scale-like creatures. These pass through several stages and at 20°C (68°F) emerge as adults about 30 days after egg-laying. Plant damage is caused by the feeding of the nymphs, which suck the sap and produce sticky honeydew. Spraying at regular intervals does not entirely eliminate them as they are resistant to many chemical pesticides. We have been told that placing a few French marigold plants at strategic intervals on the benches will solve the problem!

The biological control agent is *Encarsia formosa*, a tiny 1-mm long black and yellow parasitic wasp which attacks and kills the glasshouse whitefly. If whitefly reach epidemic proportions, rarely occurring in cool greenhouses, other controls will be necessary. Packs of the predator are available from several companies specializing in this type of environmental control. It would appear with all these biological controls that strict adherence to the instructions is absolutely essential otherwise results may be poor. This is particularly so with regard to the stage at which they are introduced and the range of temperature at the time. Once again it seems that plants under glass are most prone to attack; those moved outdoors to cool shady, conditions are seldom affected.

Slugs and Snails

These may feed on the leaves but are not a significant problem when auriculas are grown in pots. In the open ground this is a different matter and the effect of these pests seems to vary from one garden to another. In some they are a major pest and will ravage the plants, while in others the problem is insignificant. They will climb up on to benches but slugs are more of a danger if the plants are at or around ground level in frames or standing outdoors. The small metaldehyde or methiocarb pellets can be used to control them or a metaldehyde spray. Some people do not like using these pellets due to the danger that wildlife, pets or children might eat them or the poisoned slugs. They should be used with extreme care. The only real alternative is searching for them amongst the plants and hand picking.

Caterpillars

These can be a nuisance during summer, from June onwards, but rarely attack auriculas. When they do it is a problem as the plant may be ruined for show purposes. Usually hand picking is sufficient but as most glasshouse species are green or brown in colour and only feed at night they can be difficult to catch, hiding away during the day, although the signs of their presence, lacy damaged leaves, are fairly obvious. When the plants are treated with systemic insecticide, against red spider mite or aphids, any caterpillars will also be killed. The caterpillar of the tortrix moth sometimes attacks auriculas, disfiguring the plant. The small caterpillar spins the leaves

together with silken threads, feeds and then pupates in this protected place. Keeping the moth from the greenhouse by covering all doors and vents with green mesh is the best preventative.

Finally, thrips and leafhoppers will also attack the foliage causing severe mottling and bringing the risk of virus diseases. They have been encouraged by the run of recent hot summers but moving the plants outside during June, July and August into frames, or a cool north-facing spot with overhead cover, will reduce the likelihood of attack by many of these flying pests.

DISEASES

Auricula rot (*Botrytis cinerea*)

One of the most dreaded words among auricula growers is 'rot', probably responsible for the demise of more plants than all other causes combined. References to rot, and the death of whole collections of plants, are frequent in the literature of the early nineteenth century. It is still common today.

The cause of this disease is the grey mould *Botrytis cinerea* which grows on dead or decaying leaves. The fungus will invade the carrot through a decaying leaf or the spores may establish themselves on living tissue. Small wounds are vulnerable to the airborne spores and drops of water lodging in the heart of the plant, from careless watering or overhead drips, are equally likely to produce the condition known as crown rot. Once started the fungus spreads rapidly and if not immediately treated will almost certainly cause the death of the plant. The start of the disease is easy to detect as the affected tissue turns soft and black with an unpleasant odour. As it develops the affected parts are covered with a grey mould from which fine white spores rise when the plant is handled. Treatment consists of cutting away the decaying parts from the crown to firm tissue and then cauterizing with meths, sulphur, benomyl, etc. Providing treatment is given in time the plant will normally produce fresh offsets from the undamaged parts.

When botrytis attacks the carrot it is referred to as canker or hard rot. This is not the same as the natural decay that occurs on the lower part of the carrot due to age. When this happens a callus is formed, sealing off the healthy portion. Where dead tissue is present, however, the danger is that over-watering will bring on botrytis which can soon spread to the living parts of the plant.

The best remedy is to ensure that the conditions necessary for the growth of the fungus do not arise: the removal of dead leaves, an open porous compost, good ventilation and careful watering will keep it at bay.

The use of systemic fungicides like Benlate have done much to prevent botrytis from being the problem it once was: it seems more likely that the reason for most plant losses attributed to 'rot' is poor cultivation, most likely a faulty compost that has been over-watered.

Virus diseases

Until 1980 very little was known about viruses in auriculas as no original research had been done, due to the lack of commercial interest.

Some discussion has taken place on the subject but auriculas do not seem to be particularly prone to severe infection and plant losses due to virus are very rare.

In recent years concern has increased with the tendency of several varieties to show yellow streaks or blotches on the foliage. This is something that is more pronounced in winter

and the new spring growth often appears healthy, the blotches disappearing. In the past virus was dismissed as a cause and the condition put down to mineral deficiency.

In 1980 Ed Pickin, who also initiated the first tissue culture of auriculas, took some leaves of two older varieties, show self 'Harrison Weir' and Alpine light centre 'Lady Daresbury', to a friend at Birmingham University Botanical Gardens. Tests were conducted on the sap from the leaves applied to a Nicotiana species. From these tests it was established that at least two viruses were present.

The majority of viruses are transmittable, usually by aphids or other sucking insects. It would seem reasonable to assume therefore that once a virus arrives in a collection most plants would be affected fairly rapidly. This does not appear to happen so it seems that auriculas are either resistant to virus or more probably able to tolerate low levels of infection.

One of the attractions of meristem culture is the possibility of eliminating virus. Some varieties treated in this way, 'Tinkerbell' and 'Ower' are examples, have been rejuvenated although in general the process has not given the anticipated results as far as flowering performance is concerned.

The lesson for the grower seems to be to keep his or her plants as healthy as possible. When repotting or taking offsets, any implements used, i.e. knives or scalpels, should be sterilized after each plant is treated. Aphids and other pests must be eliminated as efficiently and quickly as possible and additions to the collection screened to ensure that a virus is not being introduced. It is also quite clear that the older varieties are the most likely to carry infection.

Recently a research project into auricula virus has been undertaken at Wye College,

Ashford, Kent. Work is still under way and the results have yet to be published.

Chlorosis

This is a term used to denote the abnormal paling or yellowing of the leaves. It results from the failure of the plant to produce chlorophyll, the green colouring matter. It can be a result of poor cultivation, either under- or over-watering, or unfavourably high temperatures. Generally it is caused by either nutrient deficiency (usually iron), or an excess of lime in the soil. If cultivation is not to blame for the yellowing of the leaves then lack of iron is the main suspect. This is easily remedied by watering with a solution of sequestene or Maxicrop plus Iron at the recommended dilution rates.

9 Exhibiting

The main purpose of growing the show auricula is to exhibit it, hence the name. This is also true of Alpine and double auriculas. All auriculas can be grown in the garden, though obviously some types are more suitable than others and many people grow them in pots for their own pleasure without ever dreaming of exhibiting. Those who do exhibit include many of the most skilled growers and the raisers of new varieties. The history of the auricula is bound up with that of the auricula societies who have always held annual shows as the cornerstone of their existence.

Showing is actually a very enjoyable pastime and well within the reach of any competent gardener with some experience of growing plants in pots. In the past a great deal of mystery has tended to surround the process, engendered by some past growers. This is something that has put many people off who become convinced it is beyond them. Auriculas are not difficult plants to grow although the show auricula is undoubtedly awkward and often unreliable. The task is to produce good flowering trusses and here the expert has no great advantage over the novice. It is a fact that novice growers quite frequently show plants, often varieties discarded by the experts as unreliable or ageing, in sparkling form. The secret is to grow the plants as well as possible for twelve months and if luck is with you some will be suitable for showing.

Exhibiting does not mean looking over your plants a few days before the show and then selecting. The process starts much earlier, as soon as the flower stem begins to rise. This applies to all types of auricula, including the doubles, with some variation in procedure at the final stages. It will be determined at an early stage that some plants are not going to be suitable for showing. Those that fall into this category should be moved elsewhere to provide as much space as possible for the chosen plants.

STAKING

Once the flowering stem has reached, or is close to, its maximum height it should be staked; this will be some weeks before the show. The stakes are split green canes approximately $3/8$ in (5 mm) wide; they are cut into various lengths and sharpened at one end for easier insertion into the compost. An alternative source that makes excellent stakes are the skewers sold in 100-packs for barbecues. The need for different sizes is because of the variation in stem length which is considerable depending on variety, and in some instances variations in condition.

Flowering stems will often lean to one side so the aim is to straighten them up. The stake is carefully pushed into the compost, vertical and as near the centre as practical. A small piece of cotton wool is sometimes wrapped around the stem just below the flowering truss. The stem is tied to the stake, green knitting wool is ideal being inconspicuous, although other subdued colours will do just as well. Take great care to ensure the cotton wool protects the stem. This is a fiddly and time-consuming process that should not be rushed. When tying is complete any loose ends of wool should be cut off with small scissors. Adjustment may be needed later to cater for any further lengthening of the flower stem. Some people do not like using cotton wool to protect the stem and instead cushion it by winding the green wool in a figure eight.

THINNING

Once the pips start to swell any superfluous ones should be removed to permit those remaining to develop fully. This process will commence before the flowering stem has reached its full height. This does depend on the number of pips, which on edged show auriculas can be few. Show selfs, Alpines and doubles normally have a larger number; in the case of Alpines and doubles and some selfs often into double figures. If sufficient pips are visible thinning should commence as soon as you can get at the base of the foot-stalks without damaging the adjacent pips; small pointed tweezers are ideal for this. Often the first pip, known as the crown pip, is overlarge and, providing sufficient numbers remain, should be removed. Also remove many of the small pips that crowd the centre, reducing the total to the optimum number. This process is an ongoing one that continues until the pips begin to open, when the final number is decided.

The number of pips that edged plants can carry successfully is limited; at one time three to five were common but modern varieties are more prolific. A problem with some is the size of the pips which can overlap, preventing the flower flattening. The aim is to get a nice balanced truss with five to seven evenly-sized pips. This is the maximum number most varieties can carry without losing symmetry. Five good pips are better than five good plus two middling and seven good is preferable to five. If the cultivar is capable of producing seven then aim for that. Certain varieties will produce eleven or more pips, 'Warwick' and 'Prague' being good examples. The best specimens of these plants that have been exhibited, including several premier plants, have never been shown with more than seven pips.

Selfs, Alpines and doubles are more prolific and many produce a multitude of pips that need severe thinning if the flower truss is to develop properly. Some varieties of doubles and Alpines, not usually selfs, can have as many as thirty pips. The overcrowding that this causes will prevent the flowers from ever displaying themselves fully. It is noticeable at shows that many plants have not been prepared properly; they have not been thinned out to provide a balanced truss. This has particularly been the case with double auriculas, many plants having congested flower heads due to the reluctance of the owners to remove excess pips. The object when thinning a truss is threefold: to produce a symmetrical appearance, evenly-sized pips and no overcrowding.

As the truss starts to expand and the foot-stalks lengthen the pips should be separated to enable them to flatten. The footstalks are quite flexible and can be manipulated by wedging cotton wool between them, below the level of the sepals. This will not be removed until the plants are finally prepared for the show bench at the show itself. The cotton wool, which may need readjustment as the flowers open, also helps in avoiding damage to the truss during transportation to the show.

TRANSPORTING THE PLANTS

In the past a variety of containers or boxes were used, many custom-made, for transporting plants to the show. Some have been handed down from grower to grower and have quite a history in themselves. The plants must be very carefully packed, particularly show auriculas with mealed flowers and foliage. It is very easy for these plants to suffer 'smearing' which ruins their appearance. There should be adequate space between each plant and they must be held firmly in place. Many growers use polystyrene trays which are recessed to hold pots; they can usually be obtained from garden centres who discard them after use. Newspaper or sponge rubber packed around the pots in large plastic or other containers are two alternatives. Finally, all plants for the show should be well watered the previous evening particularly if in clay pots – the best method is by immersion; it is surprising how they can dry out during a long journey. Clay pots should also be given a careful final wipe.

Once at the show find a spot where the plants can be given their final preparation for the bench. Most growers have a collection of tools and utensils they have accumulated which might include:

a small tool-box or container
fine, sharp manicure scissors
wool for tying
stakes
a selection of brushes
pen and horticultural pencil
labels
tweezers
surgical spirits
sponge and/or dust cloth
cotton wool buds.

You first obtain an exhibitor's number from the show secretary's table together with sufficient pot cards and pins. The pot cards are completed with your number and the plant's name. The pins, with attached card, are placed in the pot when all other preparations are completed. Make sure you have a copy of the schedule and understand the rules and entry requirements for each class.

The next task is carefully to remove the cotton wool using small tweezers. Any dust or other foreign matter can be gently blown off the foliage and pips. Plants with meal-free foliage can have their leaves cleaned using a large soft brush. Green-edged, selfs, Alpines and doubles can all be cleaned up using the soft brushes. This includes the edge of the pip on the greens and selfs but take care not to touch the paste; do not attempt to do this with mealed flowers and foliage. Any unwanted farina can be removed with surgical spirit on a fine-tipped brush. Give the pots a last wipe with a moistened sponge cloth.

The truss can now be given its final 'dressing', a process that varies from grower to grower but can be very time-consuming. It is possible to rearrange the layout of the pips using gentle pressure and some of the tools already mentioned. The 'dressing' of plants has been elevated to an art form and much mystique is attached to it. This can get out of hand, and attention to detail together with a little flair will produce good results: well within the capabilities of the majority.

One technique that is practised by Alpine auricula exhibitors, notably Derek Telford, is to dress the blooms so that each petal overlaps. Normally some petals have two edges in view while others are hidden – this is known as asymmetry. A steady hand is required, the aim being to create a cartwheel effect with each petal overlapping the next. Using a cotton wool bud the petal is pushed from underneath the covered edge, whilst the edge of

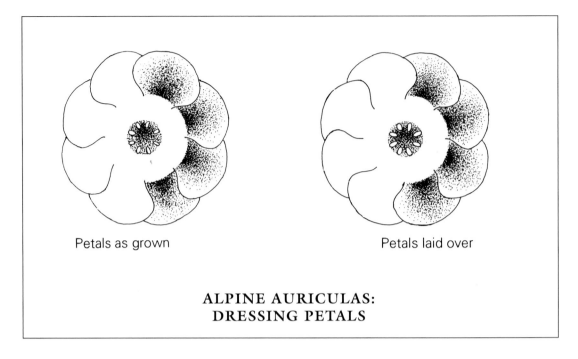

Petals as grown   Petals laid over

ALPINE AURICULAS: DRESSING PETALS

the adjacent petal is gently pushed with the index finger of your other hand. There is a danger of splitting the centre of the bloom and this is certainly not for the faint-hearted! We would suggest this should be practised beforehand on a plant not suitable for showing. Derek also uses a technique to flatten convex blooms by gently stroking with two fingers in the form of a 'V' and pushing upwards from the underside. This, carefully done, will flatten the bloom and the same result can also be achieved, on nearly open flowers, by gentle downward pressure on each petal in turn using cotton wool buds. Once all these preparations are complete you must decide which classes the plants will go into. The normal priority for the major exhibitors of shows and Alpines is to make up a six. This normally includes the best plants and should be as balanced and contrasting as possible. The plants must be carefully matched up, ideally all of the same height. This is not always attainable and in such cases

place the tallest at the back, graduating to the smallest at the front. Make sure the truss faces the front, i.e. the direction from which the judges will be viewing them.

With show auriculas no consensus exists as to the ideal combination but it might include two greens, three greys and a yellow self. At least four distinct varieties must be included and a combination of four edged and two selfs would also be satisfactory. Normally entries containing a majority of edged plants win, except in a poor year, but this does depend on the preferences of individual judges and the merits of individual plants.

The Alpines should be a mix of light and gold centres with nicely contrasting colours and again at least four distinct varieties.

Doubles are growing in popularity but the number exhibited has not yet reached that of the other types. The largest class at any of the shows is four plants. Here, in the multiple classes, a nice contrast in colours is a desirable feature.

The next most important classes tend to be either the fours, or the single classes. Those plants shown in three-plant and two-plant classes are usually of the 'second string' variety, certainly so with both shows and Alpines. This is of course a generalization which is affected by the quality of the plants each season, variable from year to year.

A serious exhibitor of either shows or of Alpines will need almost thirty plants to compete in all classes at a show; the number with doubles is around twelve. You can of course show much smaller numbers and many do. It has not been unknown in the past for someone to bring a solitary plant and be awarded a Premier. On rare occasions Premiers have been won by plants shown in the novice section.

A large selection of cups and awards are competed for at the various annual shows. Some of the cups date back many years and are awarded annually – to be held by the winner for one year. In addition all three sections present medals or spoons to the owners of the Premier plants which are retained by them.

In conclusion, exhibiting can be very rewarding, adding greatly to the overall interest and pleasure in growing auriculas.

10 The Auricula Societies

Toward the end of the eighteenth and the beginning of the nineteenth century, a large number of what were called 'Florists' societies' were formed, a 'Florist' (as defined earlier) being one who aims for absolute perfection in a flower according to fixed and unalterable standards. This is opposed to a Horticulturist who breeds for floral effect, form and standards not being unalterable, although form will be taken into account when assessing the value of plants.

Amongst these Florists' flowers were gold-laced polyanthus, carnations, laced pinks, ranunculus, double hollyhocks, tulips and auriculas.

Of all these flowers it is probably true to say that the auricula alone is in a stronger position today than at any other period in its history. The three National Auricula and Primula Societies have staged shows that, on occasion, have exceeded 1,000 plants, the majority of which were auriculas.

The old Florists' societies tended to be concentrated in the North and Midlands with some in East Anglia and London. Shows also took place in the West Country, in towns like Taunton and Bristol. Tradition has it that the auricula was introduced into England by Flemish weavers fleeing from religious persecution on the Continent. Although this explanation has been long held Ruth Duthie, a leading historian who died in February 1993, writing in the 1992 Northern Society yearbook, challenged this assumption. She thought it more likely that the plants arrived in England in much the same way that most other flowers did during this period: interchange of plants between leading English and Continental plantsmen. The writings of Gerard (1529) and Parkinson (1629) indicate that this was a common practice.

Numerous references to auricula shows appear in newspapers in the early part of the nineteenth century. The usual venue was a room in an inn with the show advertised by a copper kettle hung outside. The kettle was the main prize and was much coveted as a useful addition to the modest household equipment of those days.

Judging was by consensus, with the plants passed from hand to hand around the table. Gamesmanship was also prevalent, as was a good deal of personal animosity, neither of which is a problem today. The proceedings usually ended with a meal or 'feast', together with much consumption of ale.

In the second half of the nineteenth century, with rising living standards and the spread of railways, an attempt was made to form a National Auricula Society. The Northern Section centenary yearbook of 1971 has the following quotation:

It was resolved in 1872–3 to revive the Exhibitions of the above Society. The Middleton Florists held their Auricula

Show in 1872 and the growers of Lancashire and Yorkshire meeting there resolved to support the Nat. Aur. Society.

This, part of the first entry in the minute books of the Society by the Rev. F. D. Horner, created a mystery that remained for most of this century: that the National Auricula Society had existed prior to the meeting at Middleton. It was not until 1993 that Jim Gould, a Midland member and keen student of auricula history, wrote in the Northern year book about 'The Earlier National Auricula Society'; evidence that indicated national shows were held between 1862–5. The first show was held at Regent's Park, London, with the subsequent ones at York, Regent's Park again and finally Cambridge. The well-known gardening writer, Shirley Hibberd, visited the 1865 show and launched an attack on certain aspects including the fact that it was run by a 'small clique'. This caused the cessation of activities until the Northern Society was formed in 1872.

At the invitation of The Royal Botanical and Horticultural Society of Manchester the first show was held at the town hall on 29 April 1873. Soon after a group of enthusiasts formed the Southern Section and held their first show at the Crystal Palace in April 1876.

The Midlanders were slower than their fellow florists but in 1900 a Midland Section was formed, with the first show held in The Botanical Gardens at Birmingham. Although small by some standards the societies continued to flourish despite setbacks due mainly to the two World Wars. The Midland Section suffered a setback and ceased to operate, due to lack of support, between 1930–8. A number of the original members, who had continued to grow the plants, then revived the society and it has been active ever since.

The American Primrose Society was founded in Portland, Oregon, in 1941 and, while primarily concerned with other types of primulas, has always contained a number of enthusiastic auricula growers. Auriculas have been grown in Australia and New Zealand in recent years but this has been on a very limited scale. Although Florists' auriculas originated on the continent and were widely grown in countries like France and Germany their popularity declined and cultivation ceased early in the last century. Few if any are grown in these countries today and no societies are known to exist similar to those in the UK.

In 1986 a group of enthusiasts organized a show at Saltford, between Bristol and Bath, shortly thereafter joining with the Midland Section to form the Midland and West Section. The 1986 show revived a tradition in the West Country that had been dormant for 100 years. At about this time a group was also formed in the North East as part of the Northern Section. Currently the three societies hold eight annual shows, three of which are specifically for primulas.

More people grow auriculas today than ever before and interest has increased dramatically in the last ten years. The advent of micropropogation, helping to increase the supply of plants, has played a part in this while a number of commercial concerns now sell a limited range of plants and seed. However for much of the plant's history, certainly post-1900, commercial growers have shown little interest, due primarily to the slow rate of increase. The auricula has been maintained, and is now flourishing, due to the efforts of dedicated amateur growers. The vast majority of the best auricula varieties are in the hands of the amateur members of the three societies.

11 Auriculas in America

Apart from the British Isles the only countries or continent where the Florists' type of auricula is grown in any numbers are the United States, mostly concentrated in Oregon and Washington State, together with adjacent parts of Canada.

Auricula growing, as far as we know, died out in the rest of Europe, although it is presumed garden or border types still survive. A handful of enthusiasts have attempted, from time to time, to cultivate them in such distant countries as New Zealand and Australia but their efforts have been isolated.

References to auriculas in American gardening literature are few but keen gardeners did grow them as early as 1767, as recorded by Thomas Jefferson in his garden book. Bernard McMahon of Philadelphia exchanged or traded both seed and plants with Jefferson, importing plants from London around 1808.

For more than 100 years seeds of show, Alpine and garden auriculas have been purchased by American gardeners from sources like Suttons, Douglas, Thompson and Morgan and later Haysom. Before and after the Second World War some seed was also supplied to various enthusiasts by amateur British growers and this has continued, on a small scale, to the present day. From American commercial sources garden auricula seed has been on offer but usually produces plants of nondescript quality, much the same as most UK commercial seed.

After the First World War a small number of growers are known of, including Mrs Hayward of Maine who was awarded a bronze medal at the 1941 Massachusetts Horticultural Society Spring Show for a display of auriculas. Mrs Rae Berry of Portland, Oregon specialized in primulas, as well as Alpine plants, and raised show auriculas from seed obtained from an unknown British grower in the early 1930s. One of these was a white edge which she named 'Snow Lady'. This plant was pictured in the 50th Anniversary edition of the American Primrose Society journal, published in 1991, and apparently still survives in many collections today.

Another well-known enthusiast was Dr W. Blasdale, author of *The Cultivated Species of Primula*, who photographed plants he grew, both show and Alpine auriculas, in the 1920s. It is said that these plants were not up to 'show standard' which is not surprising as his home was in San Francisco Bay, an area not conducive to primulas. Photographs that survive of British-grown plants from this period certainly do not flatter the 'shows' either, although the Alpines were of a higher quality.

In 1941 the American Primrose Society (A.P.S.) was formed, giving an impetus to the growing of primroses and auriculas. Members began to exchange plants and hybridizing programmes commenced, although as far as auriculas were concerned they remained scarce and difficult to obtain. This of course was the situation that also existed in Great Britain at the time, with a sharp decline of stocks due to the need to grow foodstuffs rather than ornamental plants. When the Second World War ended those British growers who had managed to maintain a few plants, like Frank Faulkner, began slowly to build up stocks. This was a tortuous process especially with plants that were, in any case, uncommon due to their slow rate of increase. The real impetus in America began when contact was established with some of the stalwarts of the Northern and Southern Sections of the British Auricula Societies. They included Robert Briggs, Northern Secretary in the immediate post-war years; Thomas Meek, editor of the Yearbook, known as *Teem*; the authority on many old Florists' flowers, Dan Bamford of Middleton and his friend Cyril Haysom, the leading hybridizer of shows. Florence Bellis, the originator of the famous Barnhaven polyanthus and primrose, was the editor of the *APS Quarterly* at this time and persuaded most of them to contribute articles. Later, other equally well known growers like Dr Robert Newton, Jack Ballard and C. F. Hill also helped out and others have done so in smaller less publicized ways. Peter Ward supplied seed some years ago as well as plants of some of the best greens and greys more recently, but unfortunately they failed to survive the warmth of the Seattle climate.

Undoubtedly the influence of Bamford and Haysom was very strong in the 1950s but this did have some negative aspects. They preached the doctrine of rigid standards with strict adherence to black body colour for shows and any suggestions for change were summarily dismissed. It might be said that this was exactly what they did in England and it is possible that this 'Victorian' approach, from two such influential people, slowed

down progress and future development.

Dan Bamford was undoubtedly a most knowledgeable gardener and knew a great deal about auriculas and other flowers. His writings, although sometimes pompous and pedantic, are full of interest containing much solid sense. Dan was never afraid to speak his mind, or put his thoughts in print, regardless of the consequences. He insisted, with the full backing of Haysom, that similar standards should apply in America and presented, in 1953, an antique copper kettle on which the inscription reads 'Old Copper Kettle Trophy Competed For At Auricula And Florists' Shows in Lancashire For Over A Century'. This was named 'The Bamford Trophy' and is awarded to the best show auricula plant at the National Primrose Shows. Since no similar copper kettle is known to exist in Great Britain, at least as far as the Societies are concerned, it remains a great historical prize.

In 1954, under the auspices of the A.P.S, the Show Auricula Floriculturists of America (S.A.F.A.) was founded, soon followed by judging schools, point scores and a system of naming plants. The first chairman was Ralph Balcom with Mrs John Shuman as secretary.

By this time many plants, including many of the named shows and Alpines were arriving in America. The largest grower in the 1950s was Mrs Ella Torpen of Oregon who was able to supply plants to other aspiring growers. Mrs Torpen visited the Manchester and London shows, as did several others and presumably they obtained plants as a result. Robert Saxe of San Francisco was also a visitor, making a number of friends with whom he corresponded until his death.

The main commercial source of plants was Frank Michaud of Alpenglow Gardens, British Columbia. Mr Michaud was a French nurseryman who emigrated in the 1920s after his nursery was destroyed by floods. He started afresh and built up Alpenglow Gardens into a well-known nursery, also becoming a prominent member of the A.P.S. He imported plants from England, primarily from Cyril Haysom, and then raised his own seedlings. The first officially-named show auricula under the new rules was raised by him, first blooming in 1956. On 23 March 1962 at Seattle it was presented to the S.A.F.A Committee and named 'Frank H. Michaud'. A photograph and description of the plant: 'white edge of medium habit', appeared in the summer 1962 quarterly.

Cyrus Happy III of Tacoma, Washington, prominent in the APS for more than thirty years and the current president, registered the first Alpine auricula to be named the following year. This was 'Golden Girl', a gold-centred Alpine raised in 1958 from an unknown cross. Mr Happy is also known as a raiser of green-edged auriculas and was described in 1993 as having grown-edged auriculas for forty years; also 'one of the few who has had success at hybridizing in America'. Peter Ward met him when he visited England some years ago.

In the chapter on doubles due credit has been given to Mrs Denna Snuffer and Ralph Balcom for their pioneering work on double auriculas. Plants and seed were brought or sent to England and started the resurgence of the doubles, a fitting thank you from the New World to the Old.

The current situation in America is not as healthy as one might have expected after the hopes and plans of earlier years. This may be due to climatic problems and the spread of members, often with huge distances between them. R. E. Kartack, who lived in Wisconsin, was a member of the Northern section of the British society in the 1950s and wrote several articles. In these he frequently mentioned the difficulties faced by American growers due to the climate. Robert Saxe, another prominent member of the Northern section, made similar comments in attempting to grow auriculas in San Francisco. In fact, as mentioned earlier, the majority of A.P.S members live in the Pacific Northwest States of Oregon and Washington, with others in the adjacent areas of Canada. The cult of auricula growing seems also to be a curiously British pastime. Indeed the emphasis has tended to be on growing them in the garden rather than in pots in greenhouses. In Britain the close proximity of growers is a major factor in the continuing and growing popularity of the auricula, while climatic conditions are generally favourable. In America, however, the vast distances and extremes of climate make the exchange of plants difficult.

It is difficult to say exactly how the best American plants compare with their English counterparts. It is generally accepted that they are not as good and certainly not nearly as numerous. It would also seem that the latest seedlings being produced in England are also superior, being raised mainly to show rather than for the garden.

A keen member of the Southern Section, James Long, lived in the Blue Ridge Mountains of Virginia. Before his premature death in 1990 he sent two of his plant raisings to England. They are 'Virginia Belle', described as 'a striped variety resembling a red self but with a light stripe down the centre of each petal', and a light-centred Alpine named 'Blue Ridge'. As yet they have not been seen in competition with British plants, so no judgement can yet be given.

The fiftieth Anniversary issue of the *APS Quarterly*, Fall 1991, had a number of coloured photographs of shows and doubles but surprisingly no Alpines. The best of these was a red self called 'American Beauty', raised by Mrs Beth Tait some years ago. It looks as good as many of the named red selfs currently being grown in England. The doubles shown are 'Rapps Double Purple', 'Brownie' and 'Dusty Double'. This last is a garden auricula raised from pollen sent to Mr Happy by Miss W. F. Wynne in the early 1960s and seed from the RHS. Miss Wynne sent Mr Happy some blossoms by post so he could see what they looked like. One was 'Mrs Dargan', the old striped double, from which he extracted a little pollen. The RHS seed produced three double auriculas; we wonder where they got it? One of these was a brown-green double which was pollinated by 'Mrs Dargan'. The result was the 'Dusty Double' which – to be honest – does not look very exciting in the photograph, more of a curiosity. Also pictured is a green-edged plant called 'Peter Klein'. This is a famous plant in America, raised in the 1950s by Peter Klein, a renowned hybridizer of all types of primula. It was from a cross between two seedlings, one a grey and the other green, resulting from either Haysom or Douglas seed. Unfortunately Peter Klein died in 1957 but his plant was exhibited by Cyrus Happy, winning the Bamford Trophy. 'Peter Klein' is also the name of a hybrid between *Primula rosea* and *Primula clarkei*.

Mr Happy subsequently produced many green-edged seedlings using 'Peter Klein' as a pollen parent and photographs of several have been published in the *APS Quarterly*. Some appear, as does 'Peter Klein', to be reasonable average greens but are not up to the standard of the better UK varieties. We would qualify these comments by noting that judging auriculas from photographs is not the ideal way to make an assessment. In an article on Peter Klein the man, written in the Fall 1991 issue of the *APS Quarterly*, Mr Happy states that he sold 'Peter Klein' pollinated seed 'worldwide' in the 1960s and that some of the current British greens resemble this plant. Whether he is implying some relationship is not clear but as far as we are aware none of the leading British greens are descended from his strain, nor do we know of any hybridizer who has used 'Peter Klein' offspring for crossing.

It is to be hoped that, climatic problems permitting, the culture of auriculas in America will continue to flourish and that efforts currently underway to encourage more people to grow them will succeed.

Appendix

SOCIETY ADDRESSES

National Auricula and Primula Society
Midlands and West Section
    Secretary: P. G. Ward, 6 Lawson Close,
    Saltford, Bristol BS18 3LB.
Northern Section
    Secretary: D. Hadfield, 146 Queens
    Road, Cheadle Hulme, Cheadle, Cheshire
    SK8 5HY.
Southern Section
    Secretary: L. Wigley, 67 Warnham Court
    Road, Carshalton Beeches, Surrey
    SM5 3ND.

American Primrose Society
    Recording Secretary: Dorothy Springer,
    7213 South 15th, Tacoma, WA 98465,
    USA.

Glossary

anther the part of the stamen bearing pollen, also called thrums

auxins chemicals produced by the plant and affecting growth, similar to hormones in humans and other animals

axil the angle between stem and leaf, usually the point from where a side shoot grows

callus a layer of cork-like tissue sealing wounds on a plant, also forming at the base of offsets and the carrot when cut

calyx the cup formed by sepals, modified leaves protecting the developing bud and later round the base of the individual flower

capsule the seedpod, which drys and splits open when the seeds inside are ripe

carrot cant word for the rhizome of an auricula

china edge a fault in green-edged auriculas where a thin line of farina can be seen around the edge of the flower petal

chlorophyll the green colouring matter of plants, essential for photosynthesis

chlorosis a disorder where chlorophyll is absent from the margins of the leaf, usually caused by vitamin deficiency, especially iron

chromosome a collection of 'threads' bearing genes that are only visible under a microscope when cells divide

ciliate 'fringed with hairs', usually applied to leaves

crenate having rounded teeth, usually used to describe leaves or the tube of the flower

cockled cant name for wavy or corrugated petals

corolla the collection of petals forming the flower

dentate toothed, usually applied to leaves

F1 botanical shorthand for first filial genera-tion, normally applied to hybrids

farina the white waxy powder occurring in many primulas on leaves, stems and flowers, often called 'meal' as it looks like flour

guardleaf a small leaf – a bract – situated where the footstalks join the pedicel, larger in some varieties than others

gene a unit in the chromosomes of a plant or animal, determining one character in the adult plant, e.g. a gene for doubling, a gene for virescence

genus a subdivision of a family of plants, a collection of wild species of plants that have many features in common. Auriculas are members of the genus *Primula*

ground colour the ring of colour immedi-ately next to the paste in an edged pip, usu-ally black

hirsutin a pink-red or purple colouring matter or pigment found in auriculas and contributed by *Primula hirsuta*, changing colour according to the acidity of the sap

hetero- and homozygote see **zygote**

hybrid the progeny of a cross between two different but related species, showing a diversity of features derived from both parents. A hybrid rarely breeds true, the offspring showing further diversity

line breeding the practice of breeding from related seedlings, of recrossing the progeny of two parents, thus concentrating good genes and also bad ones

mutation a change in the genetic make-up of plants and animals passed on to future generations, often called 'a sport'

out cross breeding outside a pure line, introducing fresh genes to try to create a different line of breeding

ovary the part of a flower where fertilized seeds develop

paste the dense mass of farina in the centre of a show auricula flower, that can be washed off by rain

pedicel the individual stem supporting each flower in a truss, also called a footstalk

peduncle the main stem or stalk of a truss of flowers

petal the individual coloured parts of the flower, together forming the corolla

petiole a leaf stalk

petaloid 'resembling a petal', used to describe parts of flowers altered from their normal function to resemble petals, often found in double flowers

pin-eyed a flower in which the female style and stigma are visible in the throat or centre and are above the stamens which are lower down. In auriculas other than borders such a flower is disqualified and cannot be exhibited

pip cant name for the individual flower in a truss, formerly sometimes called peep

pistil the entire female parts of a flower, including the stigma, style and ovary

pollen the yellow powder made by the anthers, the male sex cells of a flower, transferred naturally or artificially to the female pistil, subsequently fertilizing the seed

rhizome the part of the plant where food is stored and from which the roots and shoots arise, in auriculas commonly called the carrot

scape the flower stem that rises from the crown of the plant, carrying the buds and later the flowers

species a collection of individual wild plants that breed true

stamen the male reproductive organ of a flower, being a fine stalk or filament and the anther or pollen sacs, in auriculas attached to the petals

stigma the pad at the top of the style looking like the knob of a pin, that receives the pollen

style the hollow tube joining the stigma and ovary down which the pollen tubes grow to fertilize the seed

systemic a type of insecticide absorbed into the sap of a plant, rendering it poisonous to biting and sucking insects. Systemic fungicides help to prevent fungal attack

transpiration the loss of water vapour from the leaves by evaporation

thrum-eyed a flower in which the stamens are visible in the throat of the flower, usually hiding the 'pin' or stigma

truss a flowerhead, botanically a scape, where the individual flower stems radiate out from the top of the main stem

tube the narrow channel down the centre of the flower, containing the sexual parts, the pin and the thrum

undulate wavy, usually applied to petals, less pronounced than when cockled

virescence (phyllody) abnormal greenness of petals, under genetic control and hence inherited by seedlings

zygote scientific name for an embryo or off-spring. More often used in hybridization as homozygote (only one type of any gene pair present) and heterozygote (two different types of any gene pair present)

References

BOOKS AND PAMPHLETS

Baker, G. *Double Auriculas*, National Auricula and Primula Society (N.A.P.S.) (Midland and West), 1993

Biffen, R. H. *The Auricula*, Cambridge University Press, 1951

Coats, A. M. *Flowers and their Histories*, 1956

Corsar, K. C. *Primulas in the Garden*, 2nd edn, Garden Book Club, 1952

Douglas, J. *Auriculas*, Reprinted from the *Journal* of the Royal Horticultural Society Vol. LIX, Part 2 , 1934, pp. 283–91

Douglas, J. *Hardy Florists' Flowers*, 1880

Duthie, R. *Florists' Flowers and Societies*, Shire, 1988

Emmerton, I. *A Plain and practical treatise on the culture and management of the Auricula, Polyanthus etc.*, 1816

Genders, R. *Auriculas*, John Gifford, 1958 *Collecting Antique Plants*, Pelham Books, 1971

Glenny, G. *The Culture Of Flowers and Plants*, 1861

Gould, K. J. *Auriculas for Exhibition – A Classified List*, N.A.P.S. (Southern), 1968

Haysom, C. G. *Florists' Auriculas and Gold Laced Polyanthus*, Collingridge, 1957

Hecker, W.R. *Auriculas and Primroses*, Batsford, 1971

Hogg, T. *Treatise on the Growth and Culture of the Auricula etc.*, 1812. Edition with Supplement, 1833

Jacques, F. *Florists' Auriculas and Gold Laced Polyanthus*, N.A.P.S. (Northern), 1985

Lawrence, W.J.C. *Practical Plant Breeding*, George Allen & Unwin, 1937

Lawrence, W.J.C., and Newell, J. *Seed and Potting Composts*, George Allen & Unwin, 1939

Maddock, J. *The Florists' Directory*, 1792. An edition with improvements by Samuel Curtis, 1810

Mcwatt, J. *The Primulas of Europe*, Country Life, 1923

Mcquown, F.R. *Plant Breeding for Gardeners*, Collingridge, 1963

Moreton, Rev. C. O. *The Auricula, its History and Character*, Ariel Press, 1964

Newton, Dr R. *Fifty Modern Auriculas*, N.A.P.S. (Northern), 1969

Richards, J. *Primula*, Batsford, 1993

Sheader, M., and Sheader, A. *A Basic Guide to the Cultivation and Exhibition of Auriculas*, N.A.P.S. (Southern), 1992

Smith, G. F., Burrow, B., and Lowe, D. B. *Primulas of Europe and America*, Alpine Garden Society, 1984

Telford, D. *Alpine Auriculas*, N.A.P.S. (Midland and West), 1993

Ward, P. G. *Show Auriculas*, N.A.P.S. (Midland and West), 1992

Wemyss-Cooke, J. *Primulas Old and New*, David & Charles, 1985

ARTICLES

Bailey, L. 'Breeding Alpines and Doubles', N.A.P.S. (Midland and West) *Argus 37*, 1990, pp. 44–5

Baker, G. 'Double Auriculas', *Midland Conference Report Argus 32*, 1985, pp. 55–9
'Overtures and Beginners – Taking Offsets', N.A.P.S. (Midland and West) *Argus 33*, 1986, pp. 58–61
'Ten Years of Doubles Update', N.A.P.S. (Midland and West) *Argus 37*, 1990, pp. 62–4
'Raising Doubles', N.A.P.S. (Midland) *Argus 26*, 1979, pp. 42–5
'Double Auriculas Today', N.A.P.S. (Northern) *Yearbook*, 1981, pp. 30–3

Balcom, R. 'Experiences in Breeding for Double Auriculas', N.A.P.S. (Southern) *Yearbook*, 1961, pp. 15–19

'Thrums and Pins in Auriculas', N.A.P.S. (Southern) *Yearbook*, 1966, pp. 20–2

Ballard, J. 'The Growing Pains of a Gold Centre Alpine Enthusiast', N.A.P.S. (Midland) *Argus 21*, 1974, pp. 39–42
'Fancies & Body Colour', N.A.P.S. (Midland) *Argus 15*, 1968, pp. 41–3
'Twenty Years with the Blues', N.A.P.S. (Midland) *Argus 22*, 1975, pp. 43–6
'What is a Border Auricula?', N.A.P.S. (Midland) *Argus 8*, 1962, p. 7

Bamford, D. 'Auricula Growers! Listen!', A.P.S. *Quarterly*, Vol. XV, No. 1, Winter 1957, pp. 7–9
'Auricula "Lancashire Hero"', A.P.S. *Quarterly*, Vol. XV, No. 2, Spring 1957, pp. 45–7
'Auriculas' (reprinted from article written in 1935), N.A.P.S. (Northern) *Yearbook* Pt 2, 1969, pp. 77–82
'On Reading The Year Book', N.A.P.S. (Northern) *Yearbook* Pt 1, 1955, pp. 187–98

Barter, R. H. 'Charles Turner and the Royal Nurseries, Slough', N.A.P.S. (Southern) *Yearbook*, 1991, pp. 50–4

Biffen, R.H. 'Meal' (reprinted from 1949 yearbook), N.A.P.S. (Northern) *Yearbook*, 1983, pp. 27–34
'Notes on the development of Auriculas', N.A.P.S. (Southern) *Yearbook*, 1938
'The development of the Auricula', *Journal* of the Royal Horticultural Society, LXVII, 1942, p. 187
'The Strange Story of The Auricula', reprinted from *The Countryman*, N.A.P.S. (Northern) *Yearbook*, 1950, pp. 14–17

Bond, T. 'A Matter of Proportion', N.A.P.S. (Midland) *Argus 30*, 1983, pp. 48

Briggs, R. H. 'How to Grow Auriculas', N.A.S. (Northern) *Yearbook*, 1946, pp. 34–41

Coop, B. 'The Neglected Selfs', N.A.P.S. (Midland and West) *Argus 34*, 1987, pp. 42–5
'Vigour in Show Auriculas', N.A.P.S. (Midland) *Argus 29*, 1982, pp. 31–5
'Watchet', N.A.P.S. (Midland & West) *Argus 35*, 1988, pp. 49–52

Coop, G. 'Sins of the Fathers', N.A.P.S. (Northern) *Yearbook*, 1991. pp. 28–31

Dunlop, Rev. G. D. 'Bygone Fanciers', N.A.P.S. (Southern) *Diamond Jubilee Report*, 1936, pp. 40–3
'The American Primrose Society', N.A.S. (Northern) *Yearbook*, 1947–8, pp. 24–5

Duthie, Dr D. A. 'The Selfs', N.A.P.S. (Midland) *Argus 21*, 1974, pp. 42–6
'The Green Auricula', N.A.P.S. (Midland) *Argus 20*, 1973, pp. 27–33
'The Edged Varieties of the Show Auricula', N.A.P.S. Northern Centenary *Yearbook*, 1973, pp. 107–110
'The Midland Florist', N.A.P.S. (Midland) *Argus 23*, 1976, pp. 41–5
'Root Rot', N.A.P.S. (Northern) *Yearbook* Pt 1, 1970, pp. 69–73

Duthie, Dr D. A., and Hadfield, D. G. 'The Buckley Auriculas', N.A.P.S. (Northern) *Yearbook*, 1979, pp. 200–05

Duthie, R. 'Changing Tastes in Auriculas', N.A.P.S. (Midland) *Argus 28*, 1981, pp. 43–8
'Early Development of the Alpine Auricula', N.A.P.S. (Northern) *Yearbook*, 1991, pp. 34–40
'Notes on the Origin of the Edged Auricula', N.A.P.S. (Midland) *Argus 29*, 1982, pp. 41–8
'The Origin of Edging in the Auricula', N.A.P.S. (Southern) *Yearbook*, 1991, pp. 41–2

Faulkner, F. 'Alpine Auriculas', N.A.P.S. (Northern) *Centenary Yearbook*, 1973, pp. 133–6

Gee, Mrs L. H. 'A Yank at the Manchester Show', N.A.P.S. (Northern) *Yearbook*, 1954, pp. 40–3

Gould, J. 'Goosedung & the Emmerton Composts', N.A.P.S. (Midland and West) *Argus 37*, 1990, pp. 58–60

Hadfield, D. G. 'Breeding of Green Edged Auriculas', Midland Conference Report *Argus 32*, 1985, pp. 60–1
'Breeding the Green Edged Auricula', 80th Anniversary meeting, N.A.P.S. (Midland) *Argus 28*, 1981, pp. 37–40
'Edged Auriculas – Proportion and Size', N.A.P.S. (Northern) *Yearbook*, 1992, pp. 30–3
'Green Edged Auriculas of the Twentieth Century Part Two (1945–91)', N.A.P.S. (Northern) *Yearbook*, 1991, pp. 46–51

Happy, C. 'Auriculas in America', N.A.P.S. (Southern) *Centenary Yearbook*, 1976, pp. 38–41
'Auriculas in America', A.P.S. *Quarterly* Vol. XXXIII, No. 2, Spring 1976, pp. 11–12
'Green-Edged Auriculas', A.P.S. *Quarterly* Vol. 51 No. 1, Winter 1993, pp. 21–2
'More On Auriculas', A.P.S. *Quarterly* Vol. XXXIV No. 4, Fall 1976, pp. 5–8

Hawkes, C.A. 'Noughts & Crosses', N.A.P.S. (Southern) *Yearbook*, 1969, pp. 33–9

'Striped Auriculas', N.A.P.S. (Midland) *Argus 26*, 1979, pp. 51–6
'Striped (and other) Auriculas', N.A.P.S. (Midland and West) *Argus 36*, 1989, pp. 50–2
'Those Light-centred Alpines', N.A.P.S. (Midland) *Argus 24*, 1977, pp. 41–4
'The Hill Alpines', N.A.P.S. (Midland) *Argus 22*, 1975, pp. 39–41

Haysom, C. G. 'The Case Against "Fancies"', A.P.S. *Quarterly* Vol. XV No 2, Spring 1957, p. 51
'Auriculas – The Past and Future', N.A.P.S. (Southern) *Yearbook*, 1952, pp. 11–16

Hecker, W. R. 'A Hundred Years of Progress', N.A.P.S. (Southern) *Yearbook*, 1976, pp. 42–6

Hibberd, S. 'On the Origin and history of the Florists' Auricula', *Journal* of the Royal Horticultural Society, VII, 1886, p. 191

Horner, Rev. F. D. 'Auriculas' (reprinted from articles written between 1877–9 in *The Florist and Pomologist*), N.A.P.S. (Northern) *Yearbook* Pt 2, 1955, pp. 269–325

Jacques, F. 'The Alpine Auriculas', *Midland Conference Report Argus 30*, 1983, pp. 31–2

Kartack, R.E. 'Auriculas: Off Limits', N.A.P.S. (Southern) *Yearbook*, 1955, pp. 15–17

Keen, J. J. 'A Record of the Southern Section', N.A.P.S. (Southern) *Diamond Jubilee Report*, 1936, pp. 15–18.
'A Synoptical Catalogue of Show Auriculas', from the *Garden Oracle*, about 1889, N.A.P.S. (Southern) *Annual Report*, 1935, pp. 35–41

Lester-Smith, E. 'Double Auriculas' (reprinted from 1960 yearbook), N.A.P.S. (Southern) *Yearbook*, 1985, pp. 37–41
'Double Cross', N.A.P.S. (Southern) *Yearbook*, 1968, pp. 22–7

Levy, F. 'The Denna Snuffer Story', A.P.S. *Quarterly* Vol. XV No. 1, Winter 1957, pp. 4–5

Newton, Dr R. 'All Honourable Men', N.A.P.S. (Northern) *Yearbook* Pt 1, 1967, pp. 162–9
'Red Selfs', N.A.P.S. (Northern) *Yearbook* Pt 2, 1961, pp. 201–4
'Spring Manoeuvres', N.A.P.S. (Northern) *Yearbook* Pt 1, 1969, pp. 9–14
'The Draculas of the Auricula World', N.A.P.S. (Northern) *Yearbook* Pt 1, 1965, pp. 282–4
'The Greys', N.A.P.S. (Northern) *Yearbook* Pt 1, 1964, pp. 143–9
'Winter of our Discontent', N.A.P.S. (Northern) *Yearbook* Pt 2, 1957, pp. 73–80

Newton, T. 'Raising New Selfs', N.A.P.S. (Midland and West) *Argus 39*, 1992, pp. 50–1

Nicolle, G. 'The National Collection of Border Auriculas', N.A.P.S. (Southern) *Yearbook*, 1989, pp. 45–6

Picken, E. 'Blue Selfs', N.A.P.S. (Midland) *Argus 28*, 1981, pp. 51–6
'Virus and Auriculas', N.A.P.S. (Midland) *Argus 28*, 1981, pp. 29–30
'Judgement Day', N.A.P.S. (Midland and West) *Argus 37*, 1990, pp. 46–51

'The Modern Red Show Selfs', N.A.P.S. (Midland) *Argus 26*, 1979, pp. 40–2
'The Yellow Selfs', N.A.P.S. (Midland and West) *Argus 33*, 1986, pp. 50–4
'Tinkerbell Revisited', N.A.P.S. (Midland) *Argus 29*, 1982, pp. 49–52

Rennie, C. 'Experiences of Micropropagated Plants', N.A.P.S. (Midland and West) *Argus 33*, 1986, pp. 48–9

Saxe, R. E. 'Growing Auriculas in California', N.A.S. (Northern) *Yearbook*, 1948–9, pp. 28–30

Sheader, M. 'Alpine Achievements', N.A.P.S. (Midland and West) *Argus 38*, 1991, pp. 46–7

Sherwood, J. W. 'A Classified List of Auriculas for Exhibition (revised)', N.A.P.S. (Southern) *Yearbook*, 1979, pp. 43–54

Taylor, Dr F. 'Auricula Research at Wye College – A Beginning', N.A.P.S. (Southern) *Yearbook*, 1989, pp. 38–44

Taylor, R. 'Green Edged Auriculas of the Twentieth Century Part One (1900–45)', N.A.P.S. (Northern) *Yearbook*, 1991, pp. 41–6

Torpen, B. E. 'Show Auriculas in America', N.A.P.S. (Southern) *Yearbook*, 1953, pp. 28–9

Various 'Pots & Composts – A Survey', N.A.P.S. (Midland) *Argus 21*, 1974, pp. 32–6

'Sundry Auricula Composts', N.A.P.S. (Northern) *Yearbook*, Pt 1, 1959, pp. 281–5

Ward, P. G. 'Breeding Grey Auriculas', Midland Conference Report *Argus 32*, 1985, pp. 59–60
'Breeding Selfs', N.A.P.S. (Midland) *Argus 28*, 1981, pp. 40–1
'The Greys', N.A.P.S. (Midland and West) *Argus 33*, 1986, pp. 43–6
'In Search of Excellence', N.A.P.S. (Midland) *Argus 22*, 1975, pp. 30–6
'The Light of Experience', N.A.P.S. (Midland) *Argus 24*, 1977, pp. 47–51
'One Man's Way', N.A.P.S. (Midland) *Argus 25*, 1978, pp. 43–7
'Walhampton's Children', N.A.P.S. (Midland) *Argus 29*, 1982, pp. 57–9
'Red Letter Plants', N.A.P.S. (Midland and West) *Argus 38*, 1991, pp. 56–8
'Still Trying After All These Years !', N.A.P.S. (Midland) *Argus 27*, 1980, pp. 37–40

Wigley, L. E. 'A Surfeit of Seedlings', N.A.P.S. (Southern) *Yearbook*, 1974, pp. 30–2
'The First Hundred Years', N.A.P.S. (Southern) *Centenary Yearbook*, 1976, pp. 20–9

Wynne, W. F. 'Old Irish Double Auriculas', A.P.S. *Quarterly*, Vol. XV No. 1, (Winter) 1957, p. 6

General Index

Plant Index

Striped/Fancy Auriculas